D0402840

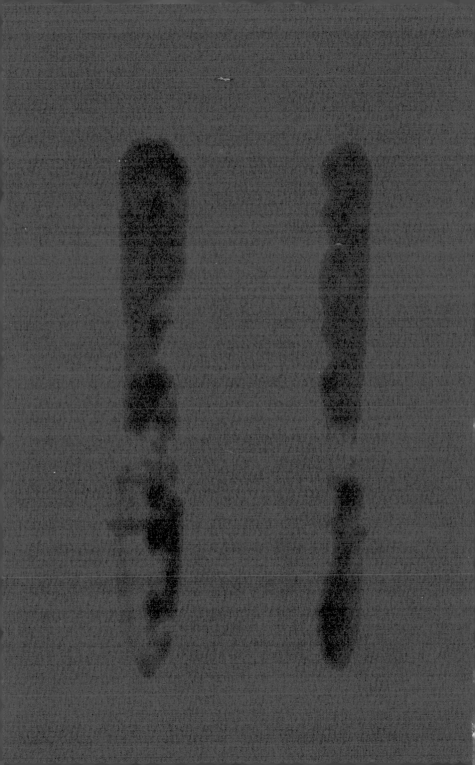

TWAYNE'S WORLD AUTHORS SERIES

A Survey of the World's Literature

Sylvia E. Bowman, Indiana University

GENERAL EDITOR

NIGERIA

Joseph Jones, University of Texas

EDITOR

Chinua Achebe

(TWAS 101)

TWAYNE'S WORLD AUTHORS SERIES (TWAS)

The purpose of TWAS is to survey the major writers —novelists, dramatists, historians, poets, philosophers, and critics—of the nations of the world. Among the national literatures covered are those of Australia, Canada, China, Eastern Europe, France, Germany, Greece, India, Italy, Japan, Latin America, New Zealand, Poland, Russia, Scandinavia, Spain, and the African nations, as well as Hebrew, Yiddish, and Latin Classical literatures. This survey is complemented by Twayne's United States Authors Series and English Authors Series.

The intent of each volume in these series is to present a critical-analytical study of the works of the writer; to include biographical and historical material that may be necessary for understanding, appreciation, and critical appraisal of the writer; and to present all material in clear, concise English—but not to vitiate the scholarly content of the work by doing so.

Chinua Achebe

By DAVID CARROLL

University of Toronto

Twayne Publishers, Inc. :: New York

To my wife
DOROTHY

Preface

The era of colonialism in Africa is almost over, but the rest of the world still seeks to impose without discrimination its own categories upon a very large and varied continent. The assumption behind these categories is that Africans desire to become members of a modern, European-style state, that the more quickly they organize themselves to this end the quieter it will be for all of us, and the sooner they will be able to enjoy the benefits of twentieth-century civilization. The only question left unanswered is the precise form of modern society they will choose. The values of the competitive, capitalistic West (or the Communist East) are so deeply rooted in our minds that an alternative African solution to the problems of the present is hardly ever considered. And yet African societies are built upon unique and traditional ways of living and thinking which have been subtly adapting themselves to a variety of changes over the centuries. The self-consciousness and sophistication of many of these societies have often in the past provided an ironic contrast to the brash colonialists, explorers, and missionaries who pushed so purposefully into the heart of the continent.

Such assumptions will not enable us to understand the problems of present-day Africa. And these problems are manifold. For in the nineteenth and twentieth centuries Europe invaded Africa and the history of the continent was radically altered. Now there was available, at first in the towns and later in the villages, an alternative way of life which Africans could either accept or reject but must acknowledge. Increasingly, the African found and still finds himself between two cultures, the traditional from the past and the European which seemed to represent the future. Only if we understand the transitions from one to the other, the compromises, the opportunities, the contradictions—both within society and the individual—can we begin to move beyond our earlier assumptions. And there are no easy answers, no simple formulations. The idea of the African between two worlds has itself become a cliché which shelves rather than diagnoses the problem.

This is where the creative writer fulfills his crucial role. Constantly questioning, testing, undermining the cliché and the stereotype, he makes his own generalizations through the particulars of his fiction. And these cannot be summarized, distorted, and vulgarized. Achebe is important here because, first of all, he has written four good novels; and secondly, he focuses his attention and his imaginative gifts upon the meeting of Africa and Europe. He takes us back into the past and re-creates the traditional life of his people, the Ibo, at the time of the European penetration and then forward to the present to the complex permutations which have arisen out of this meeting—from the eccentricities of pidgin English to the Africanization of the Church of England.

Achebe himself is quite certain that this task of re-creation and evaluation is the important one for the African writer at the present time. Recently he referred in an essay to the way in which during his childhood Nigerian dances and handicrafts, like most things African, were despised as uncivilized. This blasphemy, he is convinced, has not yet been purged. He comments:

Here, then is an adequate revolution for me to espouse—to help my society regain its belief in itself and put away the complexes of the years of denigration and self-denigration. And it is essentially a question of education in the best sense of the word. Here, I think, my aims and the deepest aspirations of my society meet. For no thinking African can escape the pain of the wound in our soul. You have all heard of the African personality; of African democracy, of the African way to Socialism, of negritude, and so on. They are all props we have fashioned at different times to help us get on our feet again. Once we are up we shall not need any of them any more.

He remains quite unrepentant in the face of esthetic objections to this educational aim:

I would be quite satisfied if my novels (especially the ones set in the past) did no more than teach my readers that their past—with all its imperfections—was not one long night of savagery from which the first Europeans acting on God's behalf delivered them. Perhaps what

Preface

I write is applied art as distinct from pure. But who cares? Art is important but so is education of the kind I have in mind. And I don't see that the two need be mutually exclusive.[1]

It is worth bearing this sense of purpose and urgency in mind for what is happening in Africa now is the result of changes and confrontations Achebe has described and sought to understand in his novels. In particular, it is difficult not to see in the pessimistic conclusion to his last novel a premonition of the present civil war in Nigeria where there is again a clash and an apparent deadlock between the traditional and the imported, between the idea of the tribe and the idea of the nation. On this occasion the contradictions between these ideas have found tragic expression.

I begin my study of Achebe's novels with an introductory chapter which examines some of the major stereotypes which Europe has sought to impose upon Africa; the second half of the chapter, in contrast, looks at the particular people Achebe is writing about and, with the aid of the anthropologistis, seeks to describe the main features of their traditional life. Here are, as it were, the basic ingredients out of which Achebe creates his novels. In the next four chapters I discuss the novels in chronological order, paying equal attention to the major themes and the fictional techniques by which they are embodied.

I wish to express my gratitude to the University of Toronto for its generous assistance during the writing of this study. I would also like to thank Paul Edwards of the University of Edinburgh who conveyed to me his own enthusiasm for African literature during those long conversations on the beaches of Sierra Leone several years ago.

DAVID CARROLL

University College, Toronto

Acknowledgments

Grateful acknowledgment is made to Chinua Achebe and William Heinemann Ltd. for permission to reprint extracts from *Things Fall Apart;* and to Dotun Okubanjo and William Heinemann Ltd. for permission to use the photograph of Chinua Achebe.

Contents

Chronology

1930 Achebe born at Ogidi, Eastern Nigeria.
1953 Graduated from University College, Ibadan.
1954 "Talks" producer with the Nigerian Broadcasting Corporation.
1956 Studied at the B.B.C. in London.
1958 *Things Fall Apart* published.
1959 Awarded the Margaret Wong Memorial Prize for his contribution to African Literature.
1960 *No Longer at Ease* published. Nigerian Independence declared.
1960–1961 Traveled in East Africa on a Rockefeller Fellowship.
1963 Traveled in the United States, Brazil, and Britain on a UNESCO fellowship.
1964 *Arrow of God* published. Received the Jock Campbell-New Statesman Award for Literature.
1966 *A Man of the People* published. First military coup in Nigeria in January; second coup in July.
1967 Biafra declares its secession from the Federation of Nigeria, May 30, 1967. Full-scale warfare begins in July.

Chronology

CHAPTER 1

Introduction

I *The Dark Continent*

THE Dark Continent of Africa has a tenacious hold upon the European imagination. From the time of Prince Henry the Navigator in the fifteenth century to the present the mind of Europe has found Africa both fascinating and repellent, the home of the fabulous Prester John and the unspeakable rites of the cannibals. Out of this ambiguity there has developed a stereotype which is still very powerful. It is most familiar as a form of landscape, as in this description of a journey into Africa in 1895:

> Going up that river was like travelling back to the earliest beginnings of the world, when vegetation rioted on the earth and the big trees were kings. An empty stream, a great silence, an impenetrable forest. The air was warm, thick, heavy, sluggish. There was no joy in the brilliance of sunshine. The long stretches of the waterway ran on, deserted, into the gloom of over-shadowed distances. On silvery sandbanks hippos and alligators sunned themselves side by side. The broadening waters flowed through a mob of wooded islands; you lost your way on that river as you would in a desert, and butted all day long against shoals, trying to find the channel, till you thought yourself bewitched and cut off for ever from everything you had known once—somewhere—far away—in another existence perhaps. There were moments when one's past came back to one, as it will sometimes when you have not a moment to spare to yourself; but it came in the shape of an unrestful and noisy dream, remembered with wonder amongst the overwhelming realities of this strange world of plants, and water, and silence. And this stillness of life did not in the least resemble a peace. It was the stillness of an implacable force brooding over an inscrutable intention. It looked at you with a vengeful aspect.[1]

This is the Africa of the European novel, with its impenetrable forests, throbbing drums, and primitive customs. It is, the clichés insist, the Africa of sudden sunsets, vultures, and blackwater fever. So alien that it can only be described in paradox, it is a desert in which vegetation riots, a gloom on which the brilliant sun burns down, a stillness noisy with threats. This is an Africa which has no meaning, no shape, no coherence. It is, in fact, the "heart of darkness"—the passage is taken from Conrad's novel— and its main purpose is to provide a convenient background for the anguish and self-questioning of the introverted European characters. "There were moments," says Marlow, "when one's past came back to one."

Most significantly, this is a landscape without figures, an Africa without Africans. There are the servants, docile and cheerful, and of course the natives who beat the drums and dance—frenziedly. These appear a few miles further up the Congo on the next page of Conrad's novel.

The reaches opened before us and closed behind, as if the forest had stepped leisurely across the water to bar the way for our return. We penetrated deeper and deeper into the heart of darkness. It was very quiet there. At night sometimes the roll of drums behind the curtain of trees would run up the river and remain sustained faintly, as if hovering in the air high over our heads, till the first break of day. Whether it meant war, peace, or prayer we could not tell. . . . We were wanderers on a prehistoric earth, on an earth that wore the aspect of an unknown planet. We could have fancied ourselves the first of men taking possession of an accursed inheritance, to be subdued at the cost of profound anguish and of excessive toil. But suddenly, as we struggled round a bend, there would be a glimpse of rush walls, of peaked grass-roofs, a burst of yells, a whirl of black limbs, a mass of hands clapping, of feet stamping, of bodies swaying, of eyes rolling, under the droop of heavy and motionless foliage. The steamer toiled along slowly on the edge of a black and incomprehensible frenzy. The prehistoric man was cursing us, praying to us, welcoming us—who could tell? We were cut off from the comprehension of our surroundings. . . .

As one can see, and as Conrad who is exploiting the stereotype to the full intends, these are not people; this is a conglomeration of limbs, bodies, and eyes, as meaningless as the forest, the river, the silence. And it is this absence of other people which declares the writer's intention. He is using Africa as a symbol, a backcloth onto which his characters can project their inner doubts, their sense of alienation. Africans in such a landscape would begin to question the clear demarcation between the observer and the mystery, between the white man and his burden. As Marlow begins to realize, this would be more disturbing than anything else: "Well, you know, that was the worst of it—this suspicion of their not being inhuman." [2] One of the purposes of the stereotype is to quell such suspicions by keeping Africa empty of other human beings so that we are free to people it with the creatures of our own imagination.

This, then, is Africa, the dark continent of the European imagination. It is an extreme stereotype, but one which clearly answers to a certain need in both writers and readers. We all require symbol, myth, and stereotype to order experience, and it is reassuring in this context to remember that African devils are white. This particular stereotype has, however, a very long history and considerable stamina. We find Leo Africanus in the sixteenth century announcing confidently: "The Negros likewise leade a beastly kinde of life, being utterly destitute of the use of reason, of dexteritie, of wit, and of all artes. Yea they so behave themselves, as if they had continually lived in a forrest among wilde beasts." [3] Closer to the present we can read the accounts of Africa left by explorers, traders, and missionaries and witness the stereotype molding and shaping their discoveries. However recalcitrant the facts, they are invariably subdued: however elaborate the social institutions the explorers uncover, Africans remain children of Nature; however extensive and well-worn the trade routes they stumble upon, Africa is described as a trackless wilderness. The genius of a Conrad or a Mary Kingsley could transcend the restriction and security of the stereotype, but most writers found in Africa what they had been conditioned to find.

This literary image is simply one of the many which cluster around the idea of the Dark Continent. It is necessary to discuss these, however briefly, since they form the background against which Africans themselves are writing.[4] The first thing to acknowledge is that Europe's acquaintance with Africa is really very slight and of short duration. Although the coastline has been known, and parts of it controlled, for over four hundred years, the interior of Africa remained virtually closed until the end of the nineteenth century. The colonial domination of the continent has been for the most part a brief transitional period. There was no great desire to penetrate into the interior. Traders were satisfied with their forts and castles perched on the edge of the vast continent, for in these depots they could gather the gold, the ivory, and above all the slaves, brought by their African middlemen. To the north was the barrier of the Sahara which had separated the civilizations of Europe and Africa for centuries. It was in the context of this deep ignorance that ambiguities and contradictions flourished.

The long debate over the human status of Africans provides an epitome of these contradictions. Although a papal bull stated officially in 1537 that non-Europeans (in this case South American Indians) were human beings with full spiritual rights, the Protestant countries of Europe were to prevaricate for several hundred years over the status of the African. At the two extremes of the whole spectrum of views were the noble savage and the depraved cannibal. The African noble savage was, for the eighteenth century, man in a "state of nature," in perfect harmony with his environment. This essentially literary view, the product of the primitivistic myths of the time, was opposed by the doctrines of perfectibility and progress which, like that of the Great Chain of Being, placed the Negro lower down the human ladder than the white races. This relegation of the African found support both from the Linnaean classification of humanity into the white, yellow, red, and black races in the eighteenth century, and from Darwin in the nineteenth. If the fittest survived, it was argued, then Africans were backward because they were inferior. Various kinds of race theory, evolution, and even phrenology joined forces with ignorance to prove too strong for the myth of the noble savage, but the essential ambiguity of these claims persisted.

It lay behind the lengthy conflict over the slave trade. On the one hand, the degradations to which millions of Africans were subjected, especially during the fearful "middle passage" from West Africa to the New World, could be justified by their natural inferiority. By mistranslating the local, domestic slave system into European economic terms, it was possible to believe that Africans were natural slaves. The abolitionists, on the other hand, playing down the differences between Europeans and Africans, stated the case for the Negro as a "fellow creature"; admittedly, he may be "fallen," but he was therefore in greater need of help. Whatever the effect upon the stereotype of the African, the slave trade had certain indisputable and devastating effects upon African societies. The widespread slave raiding fostered by the demands of Europe and America created mistrust and warfare among the tribes over wide areas. These conflicts were exacerbated by the firearms which were widely bartered for slaves and which disrupted the traditional tribal power structures. The slave trade, finally, perpetuated the isolation of the African interior well into the nineteenth century. The European merchants were anxious to keep Africa closed to honest trade and European influence in order to prevent any interference with their supply of black cargoes, while the African middlemen, their agents, were aggressively jealous of any intrusion into their lucrative markets. The over-all effect of this devastation and isolation was inevitably to strengthen the stereotype of the depraved native.

Even when the exploration of the interior began, the myths of African inferiority were so deeply rooted as to be almost unshakable. If any traces of past civilizations were found, it was readily argued from the premise of the myth that they could not be African. This was combined with the common form of culture shock in which the intruder projects upon the alien society his own fears and insecurity and then condemns it. Each failure of the alien culture to respond to recognized European values is further evidence of its inferiority.

The other great hazard of the explorers and missionaries was the Anopheles mosquito. The pursuit, the locating, and finally the combating of this carrier of malaria, the scourge of the European in Africa, is a saga in itself. The mosquito joined forces with the slavers in keeping Africa virtually unexplored for the eighteenth and much of the nineteenth century, and it added to the image of Africa another ingredient—the Dark Continent was also the White Man's Grave. Behind all the false cures and bogus theories there was the terrible uncertainty of the cause of the disease. Was it, as the name suggests, the badness of the air, the insidious creeping miasma described by Conrad as "warm, thick, heavy, sluggish," and if so why were the natives immune? In an attempt to understand what Africa has meant to the European imagination there is nothing more poignant and significant than a visit, preferably during the rainy season, to one of the dank graveyards of West Africa; there one can see recorded the number of weeks and months the newly arrived missionaries and administrators managed to survive before being struck down by the dreaded and mysterious disease. One of the unexpected effects of this in the twentieth century has been to speed up political independence for

those African countries whose high mortality rates discouraged
the settlement of privileged white minorities.

The end of the nineteenth century saw a change from the imposition of alien ideas upon Africa to the imposition of alien rule.
That was the period when the European powers carved up Africa
between them for the purposes of their own political advance-
ment. They wanted markets and raw materials for their expand-
ing economies, but above all they needed "spheres of influence,"
stretches of African territories which could be used in Europe as
the bargaining counters of power. In the last twenty years of the
century the "scramble" for pieces of Africa in the European power
game transformed the map and fixed the political boundaries
which are for the most part still in force today. The rules of the
game were laid down by the Berlin Africa Conference in 1884–85.
The main rule stated that before a country could claim a territory
it had to occupy it; and so the scramble began. The partition was
undertaken in the interests of Europe, and so the artifically created boundaries cut across tribal and economic affiliations. Some
of the results of using Africa as a European appendage were inevitably bizarre. The Europeans had to advance into the hinter-
land to stake their claims from their existing bases on the coast,
and this determined in an arbitrary way the shape of the colonies.
In West Africa, as a result, most of the ex-colonies are orientated
north-south and so do not conform to the human and physical
contours which run naturally east-west. The new barriers which
were formed in this way on the model of the nation-states of Europe cut across a variety of ties; often the only communication
between neighboring countries was through European capitals.

After the scramble Africa found itself with several types of colonial rule. But, whatever their difference, they all had one thing
in common—each represented the bringing together of two radically different, often opposed, ways of looking at power, economics, politics, reality. The Europeans in the colony translated
what they found there into the categories, the principles, the systems they had brought from the metropolitan country where most
of the important decisions about the colony were still made. The
colonized saw the local situation in terms of their traditional African cultures into which they sought to translate the mysterious
ways of the European intruders. This is the colonial condition
which institutionalizes with varying degrees of friction the imposi-

tion of Europe upon Africa. The meeting of the two cultures and the power structures in this way gave rise to a baffling variety of problems and misunderstandings. Mannoni has suggested in his *Prospero and Caliban*[5] that the two parties involved in the colonial situation fulfil each other's primary needs. The African as he emerges from the security of the tribal life which is being destroyed needs someone to depend upon; he finds such a person in the European who is rich, powerful, and immune to the local forces of magic. This desire for dependence corresponds exactly to the psychological need of the colonial European. Coming from an aggressive, competitive society and determined to succeed, for a variety of reasons, away from that society, he needs above all else reassurance. The subservience of a dependent is the easiest way of satisfying that need. The problems arise when either the dependability or the subservience breaks down.

Faced with these baffling dependents in an alien environment the European could adopt one of two opposite attitudes. These broadly correspond to different forms of colonial policy. He could insist that all men were equally rational and that, despite superficial misunderstanding, there was no reason why Africans should not be fully assimilated into the European culture he himself represented. The danger here is that genuine differences of culture are either ignored as irrational or indignantly corrected. When this fails the colonial power imposes stricter and stricter requirements for entry into the metropolitan culture. The opposite attitude is to assume that the two cultures involved in the colonial situation are mutually unintelligible. The first view satisfies the psychological demands of the rational, while the second facilitates the projection of one's obscure unconscious motives upon the subject people. This second view gave support to the idea that Africans should be allowed, up to a certain point, to rule themselves; then the "native administration" headed by the chief would be linked up to the colonial superstructure. This was the system of Indirect Rule associated with the name of Lord Lugard and expounded by him in *The Dual Mandate* in 1922. The dangers of this policy were less apparent than, but just as real as, the dangers of assimilation. Administrators tended to prefer authoritarian and hierarchical African societies because these could be fitted more neatly into the colonial system. Where kings and chiefs could not be found they had to be invented, often with dire results. In Nigeria this policy meant that the British supported and admired the status quo in the feudal and Moslem north while despising the increasingly Westernized Christian south. Often the colonial power found itself backing feudal emirs in opposition to the wishes of their subjects. Despite Lugard's warning, indirect rule was seeking to create and preserve tribal nature reserves in the midst of a rapidly changing continent. This is an interesting sidelight on British primitivism; it also uncovers the basic assumption that the European superstructure of power would always be in general control. Only when ideas of national self-determination began to gain support was it realized that feudal chiefdoms could not be incorporated easily into a modern state.

Despite differences of policy, the colonial aim was always to impose a permanent and intelligible order upon an alien society. We have seen how Europe first divided Africa into clearly defined colonies. European rationalization was now extended into other fields. Attempts were made to establish people in fixed communities with rights to their land which could be legally enforceable. Similarly, in an attempt to extend the certainty and justice of the law to all their subjects the British sought to improve and regulate African courts. This restricted their traditional flexibility which was based not on general principles but on familiarity with a stable culture. The aim of the colonial system was to make alien societies predictable so that they could be controlled more effectively; the result was to freeze social change in time and place.

The disruption caused by this imposition of alien rule was the natural element for the missionaries to work in. They were the most effective intermediaries between the two cultures and, as traditional values were destroyed, they supplied answers to the new questions that were being asked. These answers in turn undermined the indigenous cultures even further by attacking and discrediting the tribal deities who fulfilled such crucial roles in society. Inevitably there was little understanding of tribal religions and a natural tendency to label as meaningless what was incomprehensible. The missionaries, like the administrators, had an occupational need to consolidate the image of savage Africa. The more barbaric were the tribal gods and rituals then clearly the more praiseworthy were the attempts to reform and convert. The devastating effects of conversion, however, could not be clearly forecast. Converts were not simply substituting a Christian for a tribal god; they were exchanging a religion through which they were identified with the tribe for a religion without any such affiliations. This is why the security and power offered by the impressive missionary educational system were so necessary. The converts for a variety of reasons had jettisoned the rationale of traditional African life, and now they were to be given a vital role in the new forms of society which the missionaries were creating out of the destruction of the old. These forms, it should be added, were often opposed to those predictable structures legislated by the administrators.

In either case, Africans had to be educated in European skills so that colonial rule might be extended and perpetuated. As soon as this happens the original dual system begins to break down. The colonized see that the desirable things of their colonial masters are available; here is another culture within which they have been taught to move with a certain freedom. As they oscillate between these two cultures, colonized Africans come to understand with mounting frustration the limitations that are being placed upon them. These limitations whether of the individual or the state are irksome by the very standards which the Europeans brought to Africa. This is the point at which the scramble for Africa reverses itself and the prestige of national sovereignty which drove the European powers into Africa now becomes the motive for driving them out. And although the cry for national independence was not raised until after World War II, when it came it was taken up on all sides. The colonial powers who had prepared for this contingency with a lesser or greater degree of foresight, according to their different policies, had to guide this drive for independence as best they could, and finally to retire from the scene as gracefully as possible. Apart from a few remaining enclaves, all that Europe now retained of the Dark Continent was its stereotype.

II *Inside Africa*

These are the ways in which Europe has tried to make Africa intelligible and manageable. In contrast, let us take an inside view of the Dark Continent, an Africa described by an African not as a scenario for an exploration of the black side of the European soul but as a place where people live normal, unfrenzied lives. If we penetrate into the impenetrable forest this is what we find:

When Obika's bride arrived with her people and he looked upon her
again it surprised him greatly that he had been able to let her go un-
touched during her last visit. He knew that few other young men of
his age would have shown the same restraint which ancient custom
demanded. But what was right was right. Obika began to admire this
new image of himself as an upholder of custom. He felt entitled to
praise himself if nobody else did—like the lizard who fell down from
the high iroko tree without breaking any bone and said that if nobody
else thought highly of the feat he himself did.

The bride was accompanied by her mother who was just coming out
of an illness, many girls of her own age and her mother's women
friends. Most of the women carried small head-loads of the bride's
dowry to which they had all contributed—cooking pots, wooden bowls,
brooms, mortar, pestle, baskets, mats, ladles, pots of palm oil, baskets
of cocoyam, smoked fish, fermented cassava, locust beans, heads of
salt and pepper. There were also two lengths of cloth, two plates and
an iron pot. These last were products of the white man and had been
bought at the new trading store at Okperi.

The three compounds of Ezeulu and his sons were already full of
relatives and friends before the bride and her people arrived. The
twenty or so young maidens attending her were all fully decorated.
But the bride stood out among them. It was not only that she was
taller than any of them, she was altogether more striking in her looks
and carriage. She wore a different coiffure befitting her imminent transition to full womanhood—a plait rather than regular patterns made with
a razor.

The girls sang a song called *Ifeoma*. In it they said that Goodly
Thing had come, so let everyone who had good things bring them
before her as offering. They made a circle round the bride and she
danced to their song. As she danced her husband-to-be and other
members of Ezeulu's family broke through the circle one or two at a
time and stuck money on her forehead. She smiled and let the present
fall at her feet from where one of the girls picked it up and put in a
bowl.

The bride's name was Okuata. In tallness she took after her father
who came of a race of giants. Her face was finely cut and some people
already called her Oyilidie because she resembled her husband in
comeliness. Her full breasts had a very slight upward curve which
would save them from falling and sagging too soon.[6]

It may seem rather prosaic after the sinister exoticism of *Heart
of Darkness,* but this is the true measure of its achievement. Here
are the figures missing from the earlier landscape and following a
way of life which does not need questioning or justifying. The

meaningless collective activity of the frenzied mob has given place to the gentle dialectic between the individual and the forms of ancient custom. The bridegroom registers surprise at his bride's beauty, and then the traditional ceremonies intervene and conduct the participants in their chosen roles. Instead of a style heavy with adjectives and paradox we have a spare, matter-of-fact prose which records the customary sequence of events.

The appearance in the 1950's of novels like this, written by Africans and set in Africa, was not, of course, an isolated phenomenon. The emancipation of Africa from its literary stereotype is inseparable from the much larger movement towards African independence which extends beyond politics to all aspects of culture and society. One of its most exciting aspects has been the rediscovery of Africa's past, the break-through in historical studies which is gradually creating order out of the confused remnants of the great African empires. No longer can the bronze heads of Ife and Benin be dismissed as inexplicable relics from an unintelligible past. In the works of such writers as Amos Tutuola, Camara Laye, Cyprian Ekwensi, and Chinua Achebe, the West African novel also has played a vital part in this complex movement toward independence and self-knowledge.

Achebe and His Ibo Heritage

Chinua Achebe (Chin-oo-ah ah-CHEB-ee) is an Ibo who was born in 1930 at Ogidi in Eastern Nigeria. His father was one of the early Christian converts and taught for thirty years with the Church Missionary Society. Achebe was educated at the missionary school in Ogidi, at the Government College in Umuahia, and at University College, Ibadan, where he graduated in 1953. He taught for a short period and then in 1954 became "Talks" Producer with the Nigerian Broadcasting Corporation; he studied at the B.B.C. in London in 1956 and was appointed the first Director of External Broadcasting in Nigeria in 1961. In 1960–61 he traveled in East Africa on a Rockefeller fellowship, and in the U.S.A., Brazil and Britain in 1963 on a UNESCO fellowship. He received the Margaret Wong Memorial Prize in 1959 for his contribution to African literature, the Nigerian National Trophy for literature in 1960, and the Jack Campbell—New Statesman Award for literature in 1964.

Achebe has written four novels, *Things Fall Apart* (1958), *No*

Longer at Ease (1960), *Arrow of God* (1964), and *A Man of the People* (1966). They deal primarily with one group of people in one part of Africa from precolonial days to the present. Before I examine the novels in detail it might be helpful to the reader to know something of the society the author is describing. I am not suggesting that in order to enjoy Achebe's novels we need the assistance of sociology and anthropology. The novelist creates his own world according to his own criteria, and it must be understood in terms of its own inner consistency. The brief account of the Ibo way of life which follows is simply intended as a corrective to the stereotype already described and a convenient way of introducing in general terms some of the ideas I shall be using in the discussion of the novels.[7]

Nigeria, one of the largest and most populous countries of West Africa, stretches from the forests and swamps of the coast in the south to the edge of the Sahara in the north. At the time of independence in 1960 the country was a loose federation of three strong regional governments. Though none was completely homogeneous, each of the regions was the center of one of the major tribal groups—Hausa in the north, Yoruba in the west, and Ibo in the east. The territory of the Ibo in southeastern Nigeria stretches from the low-lying swampland of the Niger Delta through the tableland of the center of the region to the northern hill country of Onitsha. Although the region is divided into two unequal parts by the river Niger, it has retained a certain cultural uniformity. The Ibo are a single people speaking a number of related dialects with many social features in common.

The most important fact about the Ibo as a whole is that until very recent times they have lacked any well-defined tribal consciousness. There has been no such thing as a large Ibo "tribe" with centralized institutions and powerful chiefs. Power has traditionally been divided among numerous small groups, and the tendency is invariably toward the dispersal of authority rather than its concentration in the hands of a few people. This is reflected in the social structure which consists of countless small local communities. The basic social unit is the patrilineage which usually occupies a single hamlet made of several homesteads or compounds. Each compound consists of the houses of a man, his wives, and some of his sons; it is surrounded by a mud wall which separates it from its neighbors. Inside, each wife has her own room where she lives with her small children and unmarried daughters, and her storeroom and kitchen where she prepares the staple yams and cassava and other food. Each lineage is under the moral authority of its senior member, the *okpara*, whose staff of office symbolizes the authority of the ancestors with which he is invested. A number of lineages occupying a group of hamlets make up a village which is autonomous in most matters. In a typical settlement of this kind the hamlets are scattered along the paths which radiate from the central meeting place of the village where the shrines of the local deities are worshiped, the government of the village carried out, and the market held. Several of these villages make up what is the highest political unit among the Ibo, the village group. Such a cluster of villages would share a meeting place and be linked by common shrines and a common myth of descent.

This scattered social grouping is symptomatic of a persistent feature of Ibo life which runs directly counter to the European stereotype of the African tribe with its rigid hierarchy and all-powerful chief. There is no one who can be described with any confidence as a chief in the village or group of villages; nor is there one hierarchy of power rising like a pyramid from a democratic base to a central office. The dispersal of power among small units means that the whole body of villagers are able to participate in the running of their society at the public meetings; there, all adult males in the community have the right to express their views. Within the village itself power is dispersed among various groups, and social equilibrium is maintained by a complex system of checks and balances. This is essentially a pluralistic rather than a unitary system. The society is a dynamic world of changing equilibrium in which the individual can manipulate his social relations by balancing his responsibilities in one group against his privileges in another. For the individual with drive and ambition this provides considerable freedom of action.

In the absence of strong rulers it is rules which regulate this social order. These are not rigid and codified but in a continual process of change and examination. A law only establishes itself gradually by village consensus, or equally it may be slowly eroded by evasion and disuse. This growth and decay of the rules, the reciprocal obligations of Ibo society, is determined by ubiquitous discussion carried on at all levels. We can see here the connection

between the fragmented social structure and system of local government: rules and regulations to be effective must be common
knowledge, and the compact Ibo community is the perfect social
unit for discussion and debate. This realistic, *ad hoc* attitude toward rules and regulations can be seen in action most clearly in
the legal process where the aim characteristically is to balance the
disputing claims in order to achieve social justice. This is more
important than the apportioning of blame according to the strict
letter of the law. By observing the spirit of the law a satisfactory
compromise is usually reached which safeguards the solidarity of
the group. For it should be stressed that behind the continual
balancing of claims and the readjusting of social equilibrium there
is an assumption of human interdependence. Relationships within
society are accepted so long as they fit into the network of reciprocity which is the texture of Ibo society. The importance of such
mutually beneficial relations and the corollary that no individual
is self-sufficient are constant themes in Ibo folklore. As the proverb says, "It is only proper that the left and right palms should
wash each other so that both might be clean."

This flexible, non-authoritarian system fosters and is fostered by
the highly individualistic temperament of the Ibo. This open form
of society is also very susceptible to outside influence, always
ready to examine new ideas, and, as European contact has repeatedly shown from the days of the slave trade, adaptable in the
extreme if it finds these ideas acceptable. But, it should be added,
there are in this centrifugal system certain unifying strands quietly at work linking the politically independent villages. The most
pervasive of these is the marriage system which dictates that
women must marry into a different village from the one in which
they were born. Exogamy in this way creates a system of affiliations and communications larger than that of the autonomous village. A second unifying factor is provided by the system of titles
which bequeaths social status in the competitive, egalitarian Ibo
society. These titles are not badges of rank and authority con-
ferred by a chief or ruler as in other parts of Nigeria; they are
acquired in a certain order of prestige by the payment of initi-
ation fees which are then shared among existing members. Title
societies play a dominant role in the affairs of the community, lay
down rules of conduct for their members, and above all create a
source of unity by accepting the titled from other villages. A third

means of integration is found in the oracles and shrines where appeals to the gods can be made and disputes settled. The renown of these stretched across many communities, and the especially famous ones at, say, Awka and Arochukwu were known throughout Ibo territory.

Ibo religion transcends local boundaries. It consists of three major categories of belief—the worship of the great public deities, the cult of personal gods, and the worship of ancestors. The Ibo believe in a supreme God, *Chukwu*, who lives in the sky from where he controls fertility and creation. He is a withdrawn god, without shrines or priests, who watches over his creatures from a distance and never receives direct sacrifice. He is, however, the final receiver of all sacrifices made to the minor deities who are his intermediaries. Although these lesser gods characteristically do not form any kind of hierarchy, *Ala*, the earth-goddess, is usually considered the most powerful; she is the queen of the underworld and "owner" of men both dead and alive. Closely associated with the cult of the ancestors, she is also responsible for Ibo morality and her priests provide a powerful integrating force in society by guarding her laws and punishing offenders. In addition to *Ala* there is a great variety of minor deities, spirits of the sun, water, wealth, farms, and many others.

The ancestors are under the control of *Ala* and, represented on earth by masked men of the *Mmo* society, they act as her agents in the control of morality. The dead are part of the Ibo social world; they continue the lineage system invisibly in the spirit world and are treated, often with scant respect, as if they are still alive. The honor they receive depends on how well they reciprocate favors and safeguard the lineage against wicked spirits.

The third category of belief is the cult of the personal god or *chi*. Each person is believed to be granted by *Chukwu* at the moment of conception a *chi*, a soul or spiritual double, to which his fortune and abilities are ascribed. The *chi* fulfils the destiny which the Creator has determined and at the moment of reincarnation bargains with him on behalf of the individual for improved status in the next life. One can see here in the spirit world not only the Ibo desire for status and success but also the principle of reciprocity we noted earlier; the individual is controlled by his *chi*, but since his role in society has been bargained for he is encouraged to make a success of it.

The spirit world shares in this way many of the characteristics we have already noticed in Ibo society. There is constant interaction between the world of the living and the dead, between the visible and invisible, the material and the spiritual. Any calamity or untoward event indicates a loss of equilibrium which must be diagnosed through divination and then put right by sacrifice or by an appeal to the ancestors. The efficacy of the appeal depends, as in other spheres, upon the mutual benefit to be derived from the relationship. The one thing objected to here as in the social structure is an imbalance or lack of reciprocity; this must be corrected immediately by a realignment of forces or relations. For every force which seeks to disturb the achieved equilibrium there is a countervailing force by which a compromise or bargain can be arranged. And invariably there are a variety of ways in which the human, spiritual, and material forces can be manipulated to this end. The persistent features of this system are clearly related to the qualities traditionally associated with the Ibo—his individualism, and ambition, his tolerance and egalitarianism, his down-to-earth practicality and mistrust of authority.

This was the society with which Europeans first made sustained contact in the nineteenth century. There had been earlier penetration by the Portuguese in the sixteenth century and, during the eighteenth century, tens of thousands of Ibo slaves were collected on the coast at Bonny for transportation to the New World. But the first Christian missions were not established in Ibo country until the middle of the nineteenth century, and the British did not intervene politically until the end of the century. The Oil Rivers Protectorate was established in the area of the Niger Delta in 1885, while in 1900 protectorates were declared over Northern and Southern Nigeria. It was only then that the way of life of the Europeans began to influence the country, and several years before effective government was working in the southeast; the last independent areas were not absorbed until 1914. In that year the whole country was brought under one administration and began its history as Nigeria under the rule of Lord Lugard.

As can be imagined, the British colonial administration at the beginning of this century was baffled when it failed to find in this decentralized, segmented Ibo society the powerful chiefs it needed to exercise authority. A system of direct rule was consequently imposed in 1900 by dividing the territory into areas to be controlled by "native courts" presided over by British district commissioners with certain chosen Ibo members—warrant chief, court clerk, and court messengers. This system was deeply resented by the Ibos because the warrant chiefs were often men without status, who had come forward to welcome the imposition of alien rule. In 1918 direct rule became indirect when the D.C. was removed from the native courts and the warrant chiefs given more power; but the abuse of power by the native officials which followed led to further reorganization in 1930. Now the native courts were modified to conform to existing institutions; their zones corresponded more nearly to social groupings, and authority was given to communities rather than to individuals. There were problems and changes during the following years, but now there was greater flexibility and adaptability to local conditions. This system of local government which survived with minor changes up to Independence in 1960 fostered political integration without usurping the authority of the traditional village group.

Between this account of traditional Ibo society and the stereotype of the Dark Continent sketched earlier there is, of course, great disparity. The traditional society I have tried to describe, however inadequately, belongs to one particular part of Africa which has by now been carefully delineated by professional anthropologists; the stereotype, on the other hand, is a cluster of images and myths which has been imposed upon Africa by Europe usually from a distance and invariably in profound ignorance. The historians and anthropologists have in recent years questioned and undermined the stereotype which for so long has provided simple answers to complex questions. The West African novelists have also played their part, and it would be convenient in a study of this kind to depict these writers rebelling against the forces of literary colonialism and winning through their novels a hard-won struggle for independence. There is, of course, some truth in this. African writers have employed literature in one of its traditional roles to explore and open up new or neglected areas of experience by clearing the ground of prejudice and preconception. But such an account would be oversimplified. The main fact which confuses this simple picture is that the West African novelists are invariably writing in English or French, the language of the colonialists. We are faced with the paradox of a people describing and identifying themselves by means of a foreign lan-

guage which embodies the values and categories from which they
are seeking to free themselves.

If one wishes, it is possible to suspect this of being the most
sinister of all colonialist plots. Jean-Paul Sartre sees it in this way
in his essay, "Black Orpheus," and he recommends to African
writers an equally sinister reprisal—take over the alien language
and do violence to it. "Since the oppressor is present even in the
language that Africans speak," writes Sartre, "they will use that
language to destroy him. . . . The black poet will strip from
words their Frenchness, will shatter them, will destroy their traditional associations and will juxtapose them with violence." [8] This
may sound melodramatic and self-defeating; there are several
more obvious reasons why these African writers use and need
French and English. The chief of these is that all formal education
has been conducted in these languages for decades and so they
provide a reading public larger than any of the vernacular languages.

Achebe is aware that the African writer has been given an international language, and his statement of the problem is consequently far less extreme than Sartre's subversion:

What I do see is a new voice coming out of Africa, speaking of African
experience in a world-wide language. So my answer to the question,
Can an African ever learn English well enough to be able to use it
effectively in creative writing? is certainly yes. If on the other hand you
ask: Can he ever learn to use it like a native speaker? I should say, I
hope not. It is neither necessary nor desirable for him to be able to do
so. The price a world language must be prepared to pay is submission
to many different kinds of use. The African writer should aim to use
English in a way that brings out his message best without altering the
language to the extent that its value as a medium of international exchange will be lost. He should aim at fashioning out an English which
is at once universal and able to carry his peculiar experience. [9]

But the dilemma remains, and there is one aspect of it which will
recur in the study of the novels which follows. This is the problem
of literary convention. If an African writes a novel in English
about Africa must we assume that he will adopt the conventions
of the English novel? These conventions have developed through
the eighteenth and nineteenth centuries and into the twentieth
century in response to certain ideas and presuppositions about the

nature of society and the individual in England. Imported into the African novel and applied to very different societies and assumptions, they can easily appear bizarre. But African writers cannot escape from this dilemma, for they are expressing their vision of reality in a foreign language, through alien conventions. This is a symptom of the wider conflict which arises in society when two cultures meet, a conflict which has become the theme of so many of the novels themselves. Europe and Africa come face to face not only when Marlow sails up the Congo but also, less spectacularly, in the very form of the African novel.

There is a disturbing and still incomplete postscript to this account of Ibo society. The Nigerian Civil War which has been fought in Ibo territory for over two years has profoundly affected the lives of the people about whom Achebe is writing. Some account must be given of these confused events.

As a result of unrest in the Western Region of Nigeria following the regional elections in October 1965, an Ibo-dominated group of army officers sought to stamp out political corruption by assuming control of the country. They staged a successful coup in January 1966, in which the federal prime minister and two regional premiers were killed, and handed over the control of the country to the commander-in-chief of the army, General Ironsi. He abrogated the Federal Constitution, established a military government and, having appointed military governors in each of the four provinces, began his attempt to achieve national unity by removing what he called "the last vestiges of the intense regionalism of the recent past." In May 1966 he announced the abolition of the former Regions and replaced them by four groups of provinces. There were immediate protests from the emirs and demonstrations against the central government in the Northern Region. At some point in these confused events, the drive to abolish political corruption was transformed into intense tribal conflict; demands for secession turned into bloody clashes between Northerners and Ibos who, in the face of violent persecution, began to return to their homeland in the east. Eventually, in July 1966, mutinous units of the Nigerian Army made up of dissident Northerners seized Ironsi at Ibadan to prevent any further moves toward strong unitary government and replaced him by Lt. Col. Gowon, the army chief of staff, who formally restored the federal system of government in August.

This second coup failed either to restore order or to calm the fears of the Regions about their independence within federation. In September and October 1966 there were serious and widespread riots in the Northern Region, and many Ibos were killed at Kaduna and Kano. After some retaliation against Hausas in the east there began the repatriation of hundreds of thousands of Ibos from the north. Massacres and rumors of massacres forced them to abandon their property, their key positions in industry and public service and flee to the Eastern Region. The Ibos now began to press for a loosening of the bonds of federation; they feared that the July coup was an attempt by the north to control the whole of Nigeria, and that the northern troops stationed in the Western Region were a threat to their own independence. Consequently, Lt. Col. Ojukwu, the military governor in the east, boycotted the constitutional talks held in October 1966 and pressed for a loose confederation of regions. When negotiations between the Eastern Region and the federal government appeared to have broken down, the former announced in March 1967 that it no longer recognized Gowon as head of the federal military government.

Following the proclamation of a state of emergency throughout Nigeria, and the announcement by Gowon that the existing four regions were to be replaced by twelve states, Ojukwu declared on May 30, 1967 the secession of his Region, now named the Republic of Biafra, from the Federation. This led to full-scale warfare in July 1967. After some initial Ibo successes the civil war swung decisively in favor of Federal Nigeria in May 1968 when its forces occupied Port Harcourt, Biafra's last remaining supply link with the outside world. Although by 1968 the Biafran forces were surrounded and confined to a small area of the Ibo heartland, a mere fraction of the original Eastern Region, the federal army has been unable to break the military stalemate. Casualties in the fighting have been heavy, and the number of deaths by starvation among the Ibo has by all reports been staggering.

Achebe has been closely involved in the Biafran struggle, participating in various political missions to Europe and North America. In a recent interview[10] he has described how the problems of federation which had been accepted as a "part of growing up" suddenly became menacing. "Between May and September 1966 there were massacres in Northern Nigeria, and not only in the

North, but also in the West and Lagos. People were hounded out of their homes, as I was from my home in Lagos and we returned to the East." He feels that the origin of the conflict was the structure of Nigeria where there was "an inbuilt power struggle, and those who were in power wanted to stay in power." The ensuing political corruption created the social malaise in Nigerian society which exacerbated tribal suspicion. "The easiest and simplest way to retain political power, even in a limited area, was to appeal to tribal sentiments, so this was exploited extensively in the '50s and '60s." In this way the struggle for political power and tribal conflict became inseparable. Paradoxically, says Achebe, it was the Ibos whose leaders and intellectuals had originated and supported most strenuously the idea of one Nigeria who were viciously persecuted and driven back to their own region and then accused of sabotaging federation.

The events of recent years in Nigeria have corresponded in other words to the somber and prophetic ending of *A Man of the People* where the military coups had already begun in the novel's anonymous African state. And it is clear that when fiction suddenly became reality, Achebe's novel writing was for the time being suspended. In beleaguered Biafra his writing became of secondary importance to his role in the civil war: "What seemed important to me at the time as a subject matter for a novel seemed unimportant compared with what was happening." And yet after his resigned look at the worst, Achebe closes his interview with a gesture of the characteristic Ibo resilience we have come to recognize in his novels. Looking to the future, he is anxious to prepare for the better society which will arise from the present bitterness and conflict: "A number of thinkers feel that in this new society we must make sure that certain evil practices and abuses about which we complained so much in Nigerian society are not allowed to take root, so we have got to start talking about them now: How do you organise this kind of society?"

CHAPTER 2

Things Fall Apart

I The Village

THE most impressive achievement of *Things Fall Apart* (1958), Achebe's first novel, is the vivid picture it provides of Ibo society at the end of the nineteenth century. To the reader nurtured on the attenuated diet of individual self-consciousness and introspection, the impact of the life of this West African people is considerable. Here is a clan in the full vigor of its traditional way of life, unperplexed by the present and without nostalgia for the past. Through its rituals the life of the community and the life of the individual are merged into significance and order. This is most apparent in the village meetings which, interspersed through the action, give the novel so much of its special character.

The arrival of the ancestral spirits or *egwugwu* in the following scene is a typical example of this communal drama in which the fears and hopes of the villagers are both expressed and contained by their rituals.

And then the *egwugwu* appeared. The women and children set up a great shout and took to their heels. It was instinctive. A woman fled as soon as an *egwugwu* came in sight. And when, as on that day, nine of the greatest masked spirits in the clan came out together it was a terrifying spectacle. Even Mgbago took to her heels and had to be restrained by her brothers.

Each of the nine *egwugwu* represented a village of the clan. Their leader was called Evil Forest. Smoke poured out of his head.

The nine villages of Umuofia had grown out of the nine sons of the first father of the clan. Evil Forest represented the village of Umueru, or the children of Eru, who was the eldest of the nine sons.

"*Umuofia kwenu!*" shouted the leading *egwugwu,* pushing the air with his raffia arms. The elders of the clan replied, "*Yaa!*"

"*Umuofia kwenu!*"

"*Yaa!*"

"*Umuofia kwenu!*"

"Yaa!"

Evil Forest then thrust the pointed end of his rattling staff into the earth. And it began to shake and rattle, like something agitating with a metallic life. He took the first of the empty stools and the eight other *egwugwu* began to sit in order of seniority after him. (x)[1]

The gestures, the ritual, the formal greetings are in no sense merely part of the African local color. We approach these meetings of the clan from the inside, from the point of view of the major characters. Then in the debates which follow we witness their private fears and hopes becoming formalized in the communal decisions.

The success of these scenes is due in large part to Achebe's sensitive control of the narrative voice. The novel is narrated in the third person, but there is no suggestion of an omniscient observer scrutinizing and analyzing the customs and habits of this Ibo community. The voice is that of a wise and sympathetic elder of the tribe who has witnessed time and time again the cycle of the seasons and the accompanying rituals in the villages. This measured tone of voice implants in the reader's mind the sense of order, perspective, and harmony whose later destruction is most poignant.

The coming of the locusts early in the novel exemplifies this vital but unobtrusive function of the narrative voice. First, the narrator presents the arrival of the locusts in traditional terms, offering the reader the tribal myth without comment:

In this way the moons and the seasons passed. And then the locusts came. It had not happened for many a long year. The elders said locusts came once in a generation, reappeared every year for seven years and then disappeared for another lifetime. They went back to their caves in a distant land, where they were guarded by a race of stunted men. And then after another lifetime these men opened the caves again and the locusts came to Umuofia.

They came in the cold harmattan season after the harvests had been gathered, and ate up all the wild grass in the fields. (vii)

The narrator then moves from this larger rhythm of the generations to the rhythm of the seasons, to Okonkwo and his sons repairing the walls of their compound. Although this is a particular activity described in detail, the larger perspective gives it a

strong sense of typicality. The feeling of calm and ritual recur-
rence is strengthened by the silence in which the men work: "The
harmattan was in the air and seemed to distil a hazy feeling of
sleep on the world. Okonkwo and the boys worked in complete
silence, which was only broken when a new palm frond was lifted
on to the wall or when a busy hen moved dry leaves in her cease-
less search for food."

The cycles, the human and the seasonal, have been established.
Now they interact in the particular scene as the locusts arrive:

And then quite suddenly a shadow fell on the world, and the sun
seemed hidden behind a thick cloud. Okonkwo looked up from his
work and wondered if it was going to rain at such an unlikely time of
the year. But almost immediately a shout of joy broke out in all direc-
tions, and Umuofia, which had dozed in the noon-day haze, broke into
life and activity.

"Locusts are descending," was joyfully chanted everywhere, and
men, women and children left their work or their play and ran into
the open to see the unfamiliar sight. The locusts had not come for
many, many years, and only the old people had seen them before.

At first, a fairly small swarm came. They were the harbingers sent
to survey the land. And then appeared on the horizon a slowly-moving
mass like a boundless sheet of black cloud drifting towards Umuofia.
Soon it covered half the sky, and the solid mass was now broken by
tiny eyes of light like shining star-dust. It was a tremendous sight, full
of power and beauty. (vii)

The routines of the soporific harmattan season are disturbed but
without any sense of disorder; the people move joyfully into the
larger rhythm of the locusts' visit, the knowledge of which has
been handed down in myth and legend. The narrative voice, it
will be noticed, abandons some of its detachment and participates
in the common rejoicing:

Everyone was now about, talking excitedly and praying that the locusts should camp in Umuofia for the night. For although locusts had
not visited Umuofia for many years, everybody knew by instinct that
they were very good to eat. And at last the locusts did descend. They
settled on every tree and on every blade of grass; they settled on the
roofs and covered the bare ground. Mighty tree branches broke away
under them, and the whole country became the brown-earth colour of
the vast hungry swarm.

Many people went out with baskets trying to catch them, but the elders counselled patience till nightfall. And they were right. The locusts settled in the bushes for the night and their wings became wet with dew. Then all Umuofia turned out in spite of the cold harmattan, and everyone filled his bags and pots with locusts. The next morning they were roasted in clay pots and then spread in the sun until they became dry and brittle. And for many days this rare food was eaten with solid palm-oil. (vii)

Episodes of this kind are crucial to the success of the novel. In particular, they create a depth of perspective through which we witness the actions of the protagonists. The next sentence brings us back to these actions: "Okonkwo sat in his *obi* crunching happily with Ikemefuna and Nwoye, and drinking palm-wine copiously, when Ogbuefi Ezeudu came in." We now sense intuitively how the subtle rhythms of village life condition the characters' response to the events of the novel which are about to unfold. The detached yet tolerant tone of the narrator creates this perspective, and acts as a most effective mediator between the individual and the community, between the present and the past.

To the reader accustomed to European fiction, the modulation from the communal life of the village to the individual consciousness and back again is unexpectedly powerful. No longer is individual introspection the fictional norm as in the European novels of the nineteenth and twentieth centuries. It now appears foreign and unnatural, so that when the narrator begins to delve into a single mind we anticipate with foreboding an unpleasant turn of events. The individual seems vulnerable in his solitude and introspection; it is with relief that we see him reabsorbed into the life of the community. There, his doubts and fears can be exorcized publicly and ritualistically. This is the dimension of the novel to which previous fiction has not accustomed us—the direct translation of problems, moral, political, and religious, into public debate and action. In the episode at the beginning of this chapter, the arrival of the *egwugwu* or masked spirits suddenly transforms the workaday tempo of village life into the dramatic ritual of the public meeting. Some kind of crisis is at hand and the village needs to debate it with itself; the ritual formula is enacted, the incantatory greeting recited, and the community abandons its local differences and becomes one. Then, when a decision has been reached, the control of the ritual is relaxed, the collective intensity dissipated, and the novel modulates back to the more relaxed rhythm of the seasons and the permissive variety of village life. The manipulation of this social perspective gives an unexpected depth of implication to the events of this relatively short work. Achebe's advantage is that he is able to use with economy and confidence rituals and conventions each of which symbolizes the society he is describing. The novel in Europe, on the other hand, has its origin in the breakdown of such conventions, so that the perspective Achebe creates so effortlessly has to be reconstructed there far more self-consciously.

It would be quite wrong, however, to give the impression that the tribal society of *Things Fall Apart* is formidably monolithic. This is far from Achebe's intention. He is anxious to display the flexibility of the social structure, for only by understanding this can we understand the life and death of the central character, Okonkwo. What at first sight appear to be rigid conventions invariably turn out to be the ritual framework within which debate and questioning can be carried on. The stylized exchange between the *egwugwu*, for example, introduces a law case in which the masked spirits are asked to judge a marriage dispute. Two radically different accounts of the dispute are presented by the husband and by the wife's brother. The husband blames the interference of the wife's family; the brother blames the husband's cruelty. This is the dialectic we see in action again and again within the tribe, and the way it is resolved is significant:

The nine *egwugwu* then went away to consult together in their house. They were silent for a long time. Then the metal gong sounded and the flute was blown. The *egwugwu* had emerged once again from their underground home. They saluted one another and then reappeared on the *ilo*.

"*Umuofia kwenu!*" roared Evil Forest, facing the elders and grandees of the clan.

"*Yaa!*" replied the thunderous crowd; then silence descended from the sky and swallowed the noise.

Evil Forest began to speak and all the while he spoke everyone was silent. The eight other *egwugwu* were as still as statues.

"We have heard both sides of the case," said Evil Forest. "Our duty is not to blame this man or to praise that, but to settle the dispute." He turned to Uzowulu's group and allowed a short pause.

"Uzowulu's body, I salute you," he said.

"Our father, my hand has touched the ground," replied Uzowulu, touching the earth.

"Uzowulu's body, do you know me?"

"How can I know you, father? You are beyond our knowledge," Uzowulu replied.

"I am Evil Forest. I kill a man on the day that his life is sweetest to him."

"That is true," replied Uzowulu.

"Go to your in-laws with a pot of wine and beg your wife to return to you. It is not bravery when a man fights with a woman." He turned to Odukwe, and allowed a brief pause.

"Odukwe's body, I greet you," he said.

"My hand is on the ground," replied Odukwe.

"Do you know me?"

"No man can know you," replied Odukwe.

"I am Evil Forest, I am Dry-meat-that-fills-the-mouth, I am Fire-that-burns-without-faggots. If your in-law brings wine to you, let your sister go with him. I salute you." He pulled his staff from the hard earth and thrust it back.

"*Umuofia kwenu!*" he roared, and the crowd answered. (x)

Despite the ancient formulae, the ritual exchanges, the apparently inflexible ceremony, this is a very fluid system of negotiation. No attempt is made to extract a true version from the conflicting accounts; no principles of traditional law are invoked to apportion blame. Opposing claims are juxtaposed, and then Evil Forest uses his authority to reconcile the disputants as painlessly as possible. The peace and continuance of the tribe are the only criteria and these allow considerable freedom in dealing with internal dissension. The refusal to rely upon absolute principles of law reflects the widespread skepticism of the people of Umuofia toward authority and custom. The incident we have just examined contains an ironic footnote which underlines this:

"I don't know why such a trifle should come before the *egwugwu*," said one elder to another.

"Don't you know what kind of man Uzowulu is? He will not listen to any other decision," replied the other.

As they spoke two other groups of people had replaced the first before the *egwugwu,* and a great land case began.

Far from being the embodiment of unchanging laws, the impressive ritual is at the service of the personal idiosyncrasies of the villagers.

Such scrutiny of law and custom is one of the perennial activities of Umuofia. The villagers probe into the logic of their traditional rites to test their usefulness; they compare them with the customs of neighboring villages; and the elders recall the evolution of the present traditions from the past. We see this process in action early in the novel when Okonkwo breaks the Week of Peace:

> Ogbuefi Ezeudu, who was the oldest man in the village, was telling two other men who came to visit him that the punishment for breaking the Peace of Ani had become very mild in their clan.
> "It has not always been so," he said. "My father told me that he had been told that in the past a man who broke the peace was dragged on the ground through the village until he died. But after a while this custom was stopped because it spoilt the peace which it was meant to preserve." (iv)

Contradictions such as this must be prevented by allowing the discussion of opposing claims plenty of freedom in which to operate. And in Umuofia it operates constantly in casual conversation, skeptical asides, and formal debate. This activity is a vital part of the social texture of the community, and it is symptomatic of their openness to new ideas, their irony, and their self-consciousness. "What is good in one place," they remind each other, "is bad in another." And they enjoy testing each other's credulity to the utmost. On one occasion, Okonkwo's curious item of kinship lore ("in some tribes a man's children belong to his wife and her family") is too much for his friend who tries to outbid him. "You might as well say that the woman lies on top of the man when they are making children." The final exaggeration to which this leads suddenly introduces more disturbing implications:

> "It is like the story of white men who, they say, are white like this piece of chalk," said Obierika. He held up a piece of chalk, which every man kept in his *obi* and with which his guests drew lines on the floor before they ate kola nuts. "And these white men, they say, have no toes."
> "And have you never seen them?" asked Machi.

"Have you?" asked Obierika.

"One of them passes here frequently," said Machi. "His name is Amadi."

Those who knew Amadi laughed. He was a leper, and the polite name for leprosy was "the white skin." (viii)

The joke brings the conversation safely back home after its survey of alien customs, but before it does so Achebe has suggested with skill the curiosity and open-mindedness of the villagers, and the way in which they prepare themselves for change by exploring and assessing their neighbors' way of life. More ominously, the author has introduced the aliens, white with no toes, who will before the end of the novel exploit this openness by introducing changes which the tribal structure will not be able to withstand. But, for the moment, the society is secure, stabilized by the questioning, modification, and adaptation, which are part of the Ibo way of life.

This flexibility is seen not only in the absence of a central authority, the rejection of absolute laws, and the fluidity of village groupings. It is manifest in all areas of Ibo life. At the other end of the spectrum from the organization of society is the life of the self, and here too the reciprocal bargaining between competing claims is apparent. The Umuofians believe that each person possesses a *chi* or personal god which plays an important role in his destiny—but not to the exclusion of all other factors. As the Oracle of Agbala says on one occasion: "when a man is at peace with his gods and ancestors, his harvest will be good or bad according to the strength of his arm" (iii). This suggests that when all other claims and duties are in equilibrium, the individual is in a position to act decisively. Therefore, one is in limited control of one's destiny: "the Ibo have a proverb that when a man says yes his *chi* says yes also" (iv). But anyone who oversteps the limits of this freedom is reminded of "the little bird *nza* who so far forgot himself after a heavy meal that he challenged his *chi*" (iv). In this way, the respective claims of free will and necessity are characteristically juxtaposed without a final resolution, so that the complex interaction of inner self and external reality will not be vulgarized.

This kind of flexibility and pluralism in all areas of organization and belief clearly encourages a tolerant skepticism toward authority and custom. At the same time, it should be added, such a system precludes the directness, the unanimity, and the security

which a more static, centralized system would provide. This is the
society in which Achebe traces the career of his hero, Obi
Okonkwo.

II *Okonkwo*

From the first, Okonkwo is in the grip of his father's failure.
Unoka has not achieved any kind of status in the tribe by the usual
means of wealth or titles. He is a gentle, improvident man, most
happy when playing his flute, relaxing with the villagers, and re-
calling his happy boyhood. He is ill-at-ease when the conversation
turns to warfare or to any of the other more aggressive features of
village life; then he finds an escape in his flute playing.

Such a father need not have been a hindrance to Okonkwo's
ambitions. The tolerance and openness of Ibo society enable the
individual with drive and ability to succeed: "Fortunately, among
these people a man was judged according to his worth and not
according to the worth of his father" (i). But Okonkwo does not
see it in this way. He feels that he must succeed in everything his
father failed at and so wipe out his memory. This is the hidden
motive behind his impressive achievements, and Achebe describes
it in one of his few passages of extended analysis:

Okonkwo ruled his household with a heavy hand. His wives, especially
the youngest, lived in perpetual fear of his fiery temper, and so did his
little children. Perhaps down in his heart Okonkwo was not a cruel
man. But his whole life was dominated by fear, the fear of failure and
of weakness. It was deeper and more intimate than the fear of evil and
capricious gods and of magic, the fear of the forest, and of the forces
of nature, malevolent, red in tooth and claw. Okonkwo's fear was
greater than these. It was not external but lay deep within himself. It
was the fear of himself, least he should be found to resemble his
father. Even as a little boy he had resented his father's failure and
weakness. . . . And so Okonkwo was ruled by one passion—to hate
everything that his father Unoka had loved. One of those things was
gentleness and another was idleness. (ii)

Driven by this private obsession, Okonkwo has only one aim in
life—to succeed, and to succeed in terms of warfare, wrestling,
wealth, and status. At first, his achievements are remarkable. Despite unimaginable difficulties he survives a general farming catastrophe, and this, like other successes, reinforces his inner driving

force: " 'Since I survived that year,' he always said, 'I shall survive anything.' He put it down to his inflexible will" (iii). And Umuofia is impressed. Although the villagers do not fall into the error of believing a man is in complete control of his destiny, they are prepared to acknowledge his achievements:

If ever a man deserved his success, that man was Okonkwo. At an early age he had achieved fame as the greatest wrestler in all the land. That was not luck. At the most one could say that his *chi* or personal god was good. But the Ibo people have a proverb that when a man says yes his *chi* says yes also. Okonkwo said yes very strongly; so his *chi* agreed. And not only his *chi* but his clan too, because it judged a man by the work of his hands. (iv)

As Achebe presents this growing success, he insinuates the cause of future conflict: Okonkwo's inflexible will is bringing him success in a society remarkable for its flexibility. At first, the impetus of his fanatical ambition brings quick results; only later does the rigidity of his aims begin to upset the equilibrium of a system developed in conformity with a far less agressive concept of character. This danger first makes its appearance within the family. The traditional balance here, as Achebe depicts it, is between the masculine and feminine virtues. But Okonkwo, reacting against his father's effeminacy, simplifies this pattern and insists that his sons share his thoroughly masculine aggression and virility. "So Okonkwo encouraged the boys to sit with him in his *obi*, and he told them stories of the land—masculine stories of violence and bloodshed. Nwoye knew it was right to be masculine and to be violent, but somehow he still preferred the stories that his mother used to tell . . ." (vii). Okonkwo has created a false contradiction between strength and gentleness, and the consequences of this oversimplification are evident not only in his own tragedy but also in the life of his son Nwoye.

As Okonkwo's status and wealth increase so does his self-assertion. We sense a growing alienation between him and his easygoing clansmen as he enforces his will more and more emphatically upon his family. The incident which first dramatizes this growing estrangement is the breaking of the Week of Peace. Furious with his youngest wife for neglecting her duties, Okonkwo beats her severely: "In his anger he had forgotten that

it was the Week of Peace. His first two wives ran out in great
alarm pleading with him that it was the sacred week. But
Okonkwo was not the man to stop beating somebody half-way
through, not even for fear of a goddess" (iv). His aggressive individualism must be punished and the balance of forces reestab-
lished. Ezeani, the priest of the earth-goddess, defines his crime
and imposes the fine:

"You know as well as I do that our forefathers ordained that before we
plant any crops in the earth we should observe a week in which a
man does not say a harsh word to his neighbour. We live in peace with
our fellows to honour our great goddess of the earth without whose
blessing our crops will not grow. You have committed a great evil." He
brought down his staff heavily on the floor. "Your wife was at fault,
but even if you came into your *obi* and found her lover on top of her,
you would still have committed a great evil to beat her." His staff
came down again. "The evil you have done can ruin the whole clan.
The earth goddess whom you have insulted may refuse to give us her
increase, and we shall all perish." His tone now changed from anger
to command. "You will bring to the shrine of Ani tomorrow one she-
goat, one hen, a length of cloth and a hundred cowries." He rose and
left the hut. (iv)

Okonkwo's self-assertion has broken the organic links between the
individual, the family, and the village, and obscured the larger
perspective in which duties must be defined. (In this, he is the
reverse of his father who neglected his personal responsibilities in
order to abandon himself to the village festivals and celebrations.) Although he is repentant, Okonkwo will not admit his
error, and so opinion turns against him. He has not only challenged his *chi*, say the villagers; he has shown disrespect to the
gods of the clan.

The violation of the Week of Peace prepares us for the more
extended incident of the death of Ikemefuna. This has been in-
truded subtly but with increasing insistence from the beginning of
the novel. As the hero's early achievements are described, the narrative circles back repeatedly to the hostage Ikemefuna. The first
chapter ends its list of Okonkwo's successes in this way: "And that
was how he came to look after the doomed lad who was sacrificed
to the village of Umuofia by their neighbours to avoid war and
bloodshed. The ill-fated lad was called Ikemefuna." Okonkwo is

chosen as guardian because of his status, yet the compassionate narrative voice seems to be establishing another rhythm, contrapuntal to Okonkwo's success. When we circle back again a few pages later and witness the hero, the impressive representative of his clan, making his demands to the enemy, we experience again the same ambiguity: "And so when Okonkwo of Umuofia arrived at Mbaino as the proud and imperious emissary of war, he was treated with great honour and respect, and two days later he returned home with a lad of fifteen and a young virgin. The lad's name was Ikemefuna, whose sad story is still told in Umuofia unto this day" (ii). The feeling of foreboding is created by the double time perspective. The final sentence represents the mature, resigned perspective of tribal history which questions the more limited perspective of Okonkwo's moment of grandeur.

Ikemefuna lives in Okonkwo's family for three years and becomes a popular member of the household, especially with the eldest son Nwoye. "Even Okonkwo himself became very fond of the boy—inwardly, of course. Okonkwo never showed any emotion openly, unless it be the emotion of anger" (iv). Ikemefuna eventually feels himself one of the family. Then one day they receive a visit from the great warrior, the aged Ezeudu, who announces abruptly to Okonkwo: "That boy calls you father. Do not bear a hand in his death. . . . Yes, Umuofia has decided to kill him. The Oracle of the Hills and Caves has pronounced it. They will take him outside Umuofia as is the custom, and kill him there. But I want you to have nothing to do with it. He calls you his father" (vii). This is the dilemma the countermovement of the novel has been preparing. Loyalty to the public Oracle of the tribe is in conflict with the private loyalties of the home, and there is no chance of reconciliation. Ezeudu proposes the most humane solution—neither defy the gods by resisting, nor offend one's conscience by assisting in the death. But Okonkwo will not accept this casuistical balancing of claims. Having mastered his anguish, he insists not only on going on the journey of death through the forest but also on participating in the execution: "He heard Ikemefuna cry, 'My father, they have killed me!' as he ran toward him. Dazed with fear, Okonkwo drew his matchet and cut him down. He was afraid of being thought weak" (vii).

His inner fear renders him incapable of accommodating competing claims. He needs a clearly defined standard of conduct against which to measure his will and achievements; when he cannot find this in Umuofia, he radically oversimplifies the tribal ethic. Obierika expresses the tribe's disapproval of this literal interpretation of the Oracle when he is questioned about his absence by Okonkwo:

"Because I did not want to," Obierika replied sharply. "I had something better to do."

"You sound as if you question the authority and the decision of the Oracle, who said he should die."

"I do not. Why should I? But the Oracle did not ask me to carry out its decision."

"But someone had to do it. If we were all afraid of blood, it would not be done. And what do you think the Oracle would do then?"

"You know very well, Okonkwo, that I am not afraid of blood; and if anyone tells you that I am, he is telling a lie. And let me tell you one thing, my friend. If I were you I would have stayed at home. What you have done will not please the Earth. It is the kind of action for which the goddess wipes out whole families."

"The Earth cannot punish me for obeying her messenger," Okonkwo said. "A child's fingers are not scalded by a piece of hot yam which its mother puts into its palm."

"That is true," Obierika agreed. "But if the Oracle said that my son should be killed I would neither dispute it nor be the one to do it." (viii)

Obierika seeks a reconciliation, or at least a compromise, between conflicting loyalties. Okonkwo, on the other hand, simply wants to fulfil his duties as scrupulously as possible, and his answer to Obierika's warning is irrefutable: "The Earth cannot punish me for obeying her messenger." But Obierika is groping for a way out of this *cul de sac*, a more positive synthesis of the dialectical claims than the passive compromise he recommends to Okonkwo. The tribal ethic, however, for all its flexibility cannot provide the answer.

The death of Ikemefuna is a turning point in the novel. The guardianship of the boy was a mark of Okonkwo's hard-won status and the highest point of his rise to power. The execution of Ikemefuna is the beginning of Okonkwo's decline, for it initiates the series of castrophes which end with his death. But this event is not only a milestone in the career of the hero. The sympathetic rendering of Ikemefuna's emotions as he is being marched through the forest to his death has wider implications. At first, the narrative is detached and matter-of-fact:

The sun rose slowly to the centre of the sky, and the dry, sandy footway began to throw up the heat that lay buried in it. Some birds chirruped in the forests around. The men trod dry leaves on the sand. All else was silent. Then from the distance came the faint beating of the *ekwe*. It rose and faded with the wind—a peaceful dance from a distant clan.

The touch of regret in the final phrase prepares us for the increasing tension. Then the narrative modulates into the consciousness of Ikemefuna and the unsuspecting innocence of the victim of tribal laws is vividly portrayed. Only he believes that he is being taken back to his own people:

Thus the men of Umuofia pursued their way, armed with sheathed matchets, and Ikemefuna, carrying a pot of palm-wine on his head, walked in their midst. Although he had felt uneasy at first, he was not afraid now. Okonkwo walked behind him. He could hardly imagine that Okonkwo was not his real father. He had never been fond of his real father, and at the end of three years he had become very distant indeed. But his mother and his three year-old sister. . . . She would want to hear everything that had happened to him in all these years. Could he remember them all? He would tell her about Nwoye and his mother, and about the locusts. . . . Then quite suddenly a thought came upon him. His mother might be dead. He tried in vain to force the thought out of his mind.

Worrying about his mother, he is finally cut down.

This incident is not only a comment on Okonkwo's heartlessness. It criticizes implicitly the laws he is too literally implementing, for, as we have seen, even the compassionate Obierika is unable to reconcile the claims of the gods and those of personal affection into any satisfactory compromise. Ikemefuna has got to die. As we watch him being taken unsuspectingly on this apparently innocent journey, the whole tribe and its values is being judged and found wanting. For the first time in the novel we occupy the point of view of an outsider, a victim, and from this position the community appears cruel. Yet, the flexibility of the clan is such that we feel the antinomies, in this case, the commands of the Oracle and the inner world of the suffering hostage, might eventually be resolved. Unfortunately, there isn't time. External forces are already approaching to threaten the precarious balance even now disturbed by Okonkwo's rectitude. Then the unresolved contradictions in Umuofia will be used in its downfall. There is already a hint of this in Nwoye's reaction to the death of his friend. Obscurely he sees that cruelty is a recurrent feature of life in Umuofia:

As soon as his father walked in, that night, Nwoye knew that Ikemefuna had been killed, and something seemed to give way inside him, like the snapping of a tightened bow. He did not cry. He just hung limp. He had had the same kind of feeling not long ago during the last harvest season. . . . They were returning home with baskets of yams from a distant farm across the stream when they had heard the voice of an infant crying in the thick forest. A sudden hush had fallen on the women, who had been talking, and they had quickened their steps. Nwoye had heard that twins were put in earthenware pots and thrown away in the forest, but he had never yet come across them. A vague chill had descended on him and his head had seemed to swell, like a solitary walker at night who passes an evil spirit on the way. Then something had given way inside him. It descended on him again, this feeling, when his father walked in, that night after killing Ikemefuna. (vii)

The force of this depends upon the first-person point of view from which it is described. Coming so soon after the rendering of Ikemefuna's frightened inner world, this second relapse from the communal to the private indicates a feature of life which the tribal narrative voice is not equipped to delineate.

The death of Ikemefuna has no immediate repercussions within Umuofia. Okonkwo recovers his equanimity, and the customs of the tribe regain their unquestioned sway. The narrative, moving continuously between the daily events of Okonkwo's household and the more public affairs of the clan, integrates effortlessly the daily routine and the ceremonial by which it is articulated. We see the characters in the two perspectives of the family and the clan experiencing no discrepancy between the roles they are called upon to play. But the harmony is not complete. Achebe brings out increasingly the tensions, (which the death of Ikemefuna has crystallized) between the family and the larger community. A typical example of this persistent feature of life occurs when the priestess of Agbala comes to the village to take Ezinma, the daughter of Okonkwo and Ekwefi, to pay homage to her god. The parents' protestations are useless, and the weeping girl is carried off to the Oracle of the Hills and Caves. Significantly, we witness the event from within Okonkwo's household. We see the domestic calm destroyed by the arrival of the priestess, and we share the mother's distracted fear: "Ekwefi stood rooted to the spot. One mind said to her: 'Woman, go home before Agbala does you harm!' But she could not. She stood until Chielo had increased the distance between them and she began to follow again" (xi). And on the next day, after Ezinma has been returned home safely, we learn with surprise that Okonkwo has also been troubled by these conflicting loyalties. These tensions, endemic to Umuofia, prepare us for the climax to the first part of the novel where Okonkwo becomes a victim of the harsh laws he has previously defended and administered.

The episode is introduced by the cannon and drum announcing the death of Ezeudu. "A cold shiver ran down Okonkwo's back as he remembered the last time the old man had visited him. 'That boy calls you father,' he had said. 'Bear no hand in his death.'" Ezeudu is now about to join his ancestors and Okonkwo fears the displeasure of an *egwugwu* much more than that of the living Ezeudu. His forebodings are quickly justified. While the traditional farewell is being celebrated, Okonkwo's gun explodes accidentally and kills the dead man's son. By killing a clansman, Okonkwo has committed a crime against the earth-goddess, and so he must flee to the home of his mother. His friends console him and then must act as the agents of the enraged goddess:

As soon as the day broke, a large crowd of men from Ezeudu's quarter stormed Okonkwo's compound, dressed in garbs of war. They set fire to his houses, demolished his red walls, killed his animals and destroyed his barn. It was the justice of the earth goddess, and they were merely her messengers. They had no hatred in their hearts against Okonkwo. His greatest friend, Obierika, was among them. They were merely cleansing the land which Okonkwo had polluted with the blood of a clansman. (xiii)

Okonkwo goes into exile, and the events of part one of the novel end. For a final comment, Obierika recapitulates the painful tensions within the tribe in a way which proves in the long run to be more ominous than the temporary eclipse of the hero. Mourning his friend's calamity, he questions the dictates of the inscrutable tribal gods: "Why should a man suffer so grievously for an offence he had committed inadvertently?" The traditional answer no longer satisfies him. Obierika is rebelling against a system in which two sets of values, the tribal and the personal, are juxtaposed but remain quite distinct. An individual is punished and the tribe is safe again, but there is no organic connection between the public event and the private:

He remembered his wife's twin children, whom he had thrown away. What crime had they committed? The Earth had decreed that they were an offence on the land and must be destroyed. And if the clan did not exact punishment for an offence against the great goddess, her wrath was loosed on all the land and not just on the offender. As the elders said, if one finger brought oil it soiled the others. (xiii)

The dilemma is additionally painful because one person is frequently required to act both the roles demanded by these double responsibilities. Obierika first consoles his friend and then destroys his compound; the father of twins must become the goddess's agent and destroy them. At the beginning of the novel, this duality of roles was presented simply as a characteristic of tribal life which the villagers accept unquestioningly. It is a habit of mind which allows different orders of experience, particularly the human and divine, to be juxtaposed conveniently. No good is done by confusing the two: "Okonkwo's wives, and perhaps other women as well, might have noticed that the second egwugwu had the springy walk of Okonkwo. And they might also have noticed that Okonkwo was not among the titled men and elders who sat behind the row of egwugwu. But if they thought these things they kept them within themselves. The egwugwu with the springy walk was one of the dead fathers of the clan" (x). This involuntary mental lacuna controls the disposition of the two adjacent worlds upon which the functioning of tribal life depends.

One can perhaps see in this another example of the balancing of claims and values against each other which we noticed earlier. The main purpose of such balancing was not to create a synthesis, a unitary system which would finally reconcile all into a consistent whole, but to accommodate in terms of an equilibrium. The au-

thor keeps leading us back to this mode of thought until we come
to accept it as the most pervasive feature of life in Umuofia. And
certainly in terms of debate and social flexibility its benefits are
indisputable. But the cost to the individuals who make the mental
accommodation has not been examined. The narrator seems unwilling to scrutinize the nature of this inner adjustment. ("But if
they thought these things they kept them within themselves.")
Gradually what seems an admirably flexible and open attitude to
experience changes its nature under Achebe's scrutiny. He draws
out the inner conflict and suffering which such accommodation
exacts from the villagers. The equilibrium and adjustments of
Umuofia conceal at their center a radical contradiction between
human and divine values, and the contradiction is institutional-
ized in the role playing of the tribal officials. The antinomies of
any possible dialectic are, in other words, frozen into a static equilibrium which admits of no synthesis. The first part of the novel
ends with Obierika's baffled comment on this painful deadlock, of
which the hero himself is now a victim.

III *The Missionaries*

The muted but finely managed second part of the novel describes Okonkwo's seven-year exile in Mbanta with his mother's
kinsmen. He remains the focus of our attention and yet, since he is
a stranger in this new clan, he is no longer in the center of the
stage. Impotently he watches and criticizes the turn of events
both here and at home in Umuofia. The two threads of narrative
are kept parallel by the annual visits of Obierika.

The significance of this central section of the novel is suggested
by the two formal speeches which open and close it. First,
Uchendu, the brother of Okonkwo's mother, reprimands
Okonkwo for being so resigned and gloomy over his expulsion. He
questions him on the role of the mother in the clan. Why is a
woman taken home to be buried with her kinsmen? Why is
Okonkwo exiled to his mother's village after being expelled from
his own? These questions, which Okonkwo is unable to answer,
stress the importance of the mother in the family, the village, and
the clan—and even beyond to the web of relations which links
clan to clan. Uchendu is developing an attack upon Okonkwo's
dangerous oversimplification of the tribal ethic. He sees that his
nephew's despair is the result of the obsessive and narrow-minded

pursuit of status; when this has been thwarted by factors outside
his control, he has nothing else to live for. Uchendu seeks to redress the balance by reminding him of the maternal virtues within
the family which are as essential as the aggressive, male values by
which Okonkwo lives.

It's true that a child belongs to its father. But when a father beats his
child, it seeks sympathy in its mother's hut. A man belongs to his fatherland when things are good and life is sweet. But when there is sorrow
and bitterness he finds refuge in his motherland. Your mother is there
to protect you. She is buried there. And that is why we say that mother
is supreme. Is it right that you, Okonkwo, should bring to your mother
a heavy face and refuse to be comforted? Be careful or you may dis-
please the dead. Your duty is to comfort your wives and children and
take them back to your fatherland after seven years. But if you allow
sorrow to weigh you down and kill you, they will all die in exile. . . .
If you think you are the greatest sufferer in the world ask my daughter,
Akueni, how many twins she has borne and thrown away. Have you not
heard the song they sing when a woman dies?

> "For whom is it well, for whom is it well?
> There is no one for whom it is well."

I have no more to say to you. (xiv)

Uchendu's reprimand shows the limitations of the pursuit of success and status. Suffering and sorrow are an integral part of life,
however meticulously one obeys the dictates of the gods. Therefore, it is the height of folly to ignore the female, maternal side of
the tribal ethic, for this provides the comfort and sympathy which
alleviate the suffering caused by the contradictions and injustices
of life. In this way a characteristic equilibrium can be maintained.

The second speech, which brings to an end this section of the
novel, is very different in tone. One of the elders of Mbanta
thanks Okonkwo formally for the feast he has given to celebrate
the end of his exile: "It is good in these days when the younger
generation consider themselves wiser than their sires to see a man
doing things in the grand, old way." It seems that Okonkwo has
come to terms with his exile and that once again, here among his
mother's kinsmen, he is fulfilling all his duties punctiliously. But
there is another more disturbing reason for the change of attitude
toward Okonkwo in Mbanta:

"You may ask why I am saying all this. I say it because I fear for the younger generation, for you people." He waved his arm where most of the young men sat. "As for me, I have only a short while to live, and so have Uchendu and Unachukwu and Emefo. But I fear for you young people because you do not understand how strong is the bond of kinship. You do not know what it is to speak with one voice. And what is the result? An abominable religion has settled among you. A man can now leave his father and his brothers. He can curse the gods of his fathers and ancestors, like a hunter's dog that suddenly goes mad and turns on his master. I fear for you; I fear for the clan." He turned again to Okonkwo and said, "Thank you for calling us together." (xix)

This is the real reason for the change of tone. Between these two speeches, a new religion has come to Mbanta and begun to destroy the traditional culture. Now the elders are not concerned merely with the balancing of values within the tribe, for their whole way of life is threatened. In this crisis, Okonkwo's inflexible adherence to the letter of the law makes him an inevitable defender of the beleaguered clan. He replies to neither of the speeches; as the reprimand turns to eulogy one imagines that his silence is that of self-justification.

The arrival of Christianity in this part of Africa is managed by Achebe with subtlety and detachment. There is no dramatic confrontation, no sudden conversion. Obierika brings news of the murder of a missionary in Abame and the subsequent punishment of the clan. The startling piece of information is discussed and analyzed. For some, Abame acted wrongly in killing the missionary; in Okonkwo's opinion they were foolish not to prepare themselves for reprisals; others can hardly believe the events are true. Perhaps Uchendu represents best the point of view we have come to associate with traditional Ibo society: "There is no story that is not true. . . . The world has no end, and what is good among one people is an abomination with others. We have albinos among us. Do you not think that they came to our clan by mistake, that they have strayed from their way to a land where everybody is like them?" (xv). This fatal ability to acknowledge alien forms of life prevents any clear-cut conflict. It is this which makes the tribe so vulnerable. By the time of Obierika's next visit to Mbanta, the missionaries have penetrated to Umuofia and are using it as a center of their religion. But again there is no sense of urgency, for the early converts are merely the despised and worthless members

of the village. "Chielo, the priestess of Agbala, called the converts
the excrement of the clan, and the new faith was a mad dog that
had come to eat it up" (xvi). The only disturbing piece of news is
that Nwoye has joined the converts.

The first white missionary to come to Mbanta is greeted with
ironical good humor by the villagers. They are amused by the
strange Ibo dialect spoken by his interpreter and, as they weave
jokes around his oddities of speech, they seem unaware of the
uncompromising doctrine that is being preached: "He told them
that the true God lived on high and that all men when they died
went before Him for judgment. Evil men and all the heathen who
in their blindness bowed to wood and stone were thrown into a
fire that burned like palm-oil" (xvi). They laugh derisively at the
missionary's dismissal of their most powerful gods; this is not the
subtle dialectic they are accustomed to. But the biggest joke of all
is provided by the doctrine of the Trinity, and even Okonkwo
joins in the debate at this point: "You told us with your own
mouth that there was only one god. Now you talk about his son.
He must have a wife, then." As he goes off to tap his afternoon's
palm-wine he is convinced the missionary is mad. The Umuofians,
we feel, are justifiably skeptical toward the new religion which is
being imported in this gauche and complacent manner into the
midst of their self-conscious society.

But not everything is greeted with laughter and incredulity.
There is one point in this meeting of religions when the missionaries cease their blunt attacks and, relying upon the emotional
appeal of their message, sing a hymn:

Then the missionaries burst into song. It was one of those gay and
rollicking tunes of evangelism which had the power of plucking at
silent and dusty chords in the heart of an Ibo man. The interpreter
explained each verse to the audience, some of whom now stood en-
thralled. It was a story of brothers who lived in darkness and in fear,
ignorant of the love of God. It told of one sheep out on the hills, away
from the gates of God and from the tender shepherd's care. (xvi)

The Christian god cannot rival the great Chukwu in power, but in
his loving, personal care for the individual he appeals to all the
unresolved fears of Umuofia. He can break the deadlock between
divine law and personal affection which has caused so much an-

guish in the clan. This is the god who has captivated Nwoye still
in rebellion against his father's harsh and rigid literalism:

It was not the mad logic of the Trinity that captivated him. He did not
understand it. It was the poetry of the new religion, something felt in
the marrow. The hymn about brothers who sat in darkness and in fear
seemed to answer a vague and persistent question that haunted his
young soul—the question of the twins crying in the bush and the question of Ikemefuna who was killed. He felt a relief within as the hymn
poured into his parched soul. The words of the hymn were like the
drops of frozen rain melting on the dry palate of the panting earth.
Nwoye's callow mind was greatly puzzled. (xvi)

This is how Christianity makes its inroads in the novel. Not by a
frontal attack, backed by the colonizing forces, but by respond-
ing clearly to a need so deeply felt that it has not been clearly
formulated. Then, upon this appeal it extends its power by a logical yet almost indiscernible process of erosion.

   First, as a macabre joke, the eager missionaries are allowed to
build a church in the "evil forest," the "dumping-ground for the
potent fetishes of great medicine-men when they died" (xvii).
When they have not been killed in the expected four days by the
forces of darkness, the Christians have won their first victory.
Then the outcasts or *osu*, the tabooed slaves dedicated to the various deities, shave off their long, tangled hair, and go over to the
new religion. When the missionaries accept them into full mem-
bership of the church, Ibo egalitarianism has been challenged and
surpassed. Finally, the new converts, becoming more aggressive
as their numbers increase, are rumored to have killed Mbanta's
sacred python. In the debate which follows, the dilemma of the
tribe becomes apparent. Should Umuofia punish the converts on
behalf of its gods? "If we put ourselves between the god and his
victim we may receive blows intended for the offender" (xviii).
And the white man, they are aware, has brought not only a religion but a government to protect the converts. But most perplexing of all is the deep-seated conviction that the converts are still
members of the tribe: "No one could kill them without having to
flee from the clan, for in spite of their worthlessness they still belonged to the clan" (xviii). Okonkwo wants to solve Mbanta's
dilemma in his usual way—whip the Christians out of the village.
But the elders, troubled by the implications of such a course of

action, finally compromise and decide to ostracize the converts. Umuofia is baffled because it is being challenged by a religion quite different from its own. The villagers' religion is inseparable from the tribe which stretches back through countless generations of ancestors; for them, rival religions are not possible and conversion is meaningless. Now they are confronted by a religion with the opposite premise: they are all, like the white man, sons of God and equal in his sight. Priority has shifted from the tribe and its continuance to the salvation of the individual and, as Okonkwo muses bitterly over his son's defection, we catch a glimpse of the terrible consequences of this to Umuofia.

Now that he had time to think of it, his son's crime stood out in its stark enormity. To abandon the gods of one's father and go about with a lot of effeminate men clucking like old hens was the very depth of abomination. Suppose when he died all his male children decided to follow Nwoye's steps and abandon their ancestors? Okonkwo felt a cold shudder run through him at the terrible prospect, like the prospect of annihiliation. He saw himself and his fathers crowding round their ancestral shrine waiting in vain for worship and sacrifice and finding nothing but ashes of bygone days, and his children the while praying to the white man's god. (xvii)

Such neglect is a tribal vision of hell, and it underlines the vulnerability of Umuofia. As soon as one link in the elaborate network of tribal affiliations or in the carefully preserved chain of ancestors is broken, then confusion and annihilation quickly follow. As Obierika says, with clear hindsight: "The white man is very clever. He came quietly and peaceably with his religion. We were amused at his foolishness and allowed him to stay. Now he has won our brothers, and our clan can no longer act like one. He has put a knife on the things that held us together and we have fallen apart" (xx).

The rapid changes which have taken place in Umuofia destroy the triumph of Okonkwo's return from exile in part three of the novel. Not only has the new religion grown in strength, the Europeans have also brought their own form of government, and increased trade in the area. "The white man had indeed brought a lunatic religion, but he had also built a trading store and for the first time palm-oil and kernel became things of great price, and much money flowed into Umuofia" (xxi). Matters of principle can, if necessary, be sacrificed to this obvious good, especially if the missionaries are prepared to proselytize inoffensively. Mr. Brown, the white missionary, accepts this truce and "came to be respected even by the clan, because he trod softly on its faith" (xxi). His acute discussions with the elder Akunna clearly define the crucial differences between these rival religions and make Brown realize that he cannot win by a frontal attack. He goes to work by building a school and hospital in Umuofia and by convincing them that: "If Umuofia failed to send her children to the school, strangers would come from other places to rule them" (xxi).

Unfortunately, Brown falls ill and his successor rejects the policy of mutual accommodation. He is a literalist, as adamant and authoritarian in his beliefs as Okonkwo. The Reverend James Smith translates the complex situation he inherits from his predecessor into the extreme and inapplicable imagery of the Bible: "He saw things as black and white. And black was evil. He saw the world as a battlefield in which the children of light were locked in mortal conflict with the sons of darkness. He spoke in his sermons about sheep and goats and about wheat and tares. He believed in slaying the prophets of Baal" (xxii). Now there is no negotiation between rival myths. Smith is an Old Testament prophet, dealing in clear-cut antitheses, who divides the tribe with its elaborate affiliations into the simple categories of his creed. Unlike Brown, he stresses the exclusiveness of Christianity to the baffled villagers: "Our Lord Himself stressed the importance of fewness. Narrow is the way and few the number" (xxii). This aggressive challenge to the community draws the lines of battle and only the occasion for conflict is needed. This is provided by Enoch, the son of the snake-priest and a recent convert, who unmasks in public one of the *egwugwu* and so strikes at the heart of the clan. The mask of the *egwugwu* epitomizes, as we have seen, the duality of roles by which the inscrutable world of the gods and the human world are uneasily accommodated. Enoch's action challenges this strategy. "Enoch had killed an ancestral spirit, and Umuofia was thrown into confusion" (xxii).

Achebe achieves a fine equilibrium of approval and regret at this turning point in the novel. We have witnessed the cruelty and suffering which is part of the life of Umuofia, and yet we share their sense of outrage at this unprovoked attack upon their tradi-

tional values. This is the last of the communal scenes which have
been such an impressive feature of the novel. With the encroachments of Christianity they have become less frequent and unani-
mous. The tribal narrative voice which spoke with sympathy and
authority in the earlier days of Umuofia has gradually become less
confident and inclusive, merely reporting the different points of
view of the rival groups. But now it seeks to recapture its old tone
of voice:

That night the Mother of the Spirits walked the length and breadth
of the clan, weeping for her murdered son. It was a terrible night. Not
even the oldest man in Umuofia had ever heard such a strange and
fearful sound, and it was never to be heard again. It seemed as if the
very soul of the tribe wept for a great evil that was coming—its own
death.
    On the next day all the masked *egwugwu* of Umuofia assembled in
the market-place. They came from all the quarters of the clan and
even from the neighbouring villages. The dreaded Otakagu came from
Imo, and Ekwensu, dangling a white cock, arrived from Uli. It was a
terrible gathering. The eerie voices of countless spirits, the bells that
clattered behind some of them, and the clash of matchets as they ran
forwards and backwards and saluted one another, sent tremors of fear
into every heart. For the first time in living memory the sacred bull-
roarer was heard in broad daylight. (xxii)

The tribe has rallied only to celebrate its own demise. The narrative voice falters as it describes the unique act of rebellion, and
then assumes a new and impersonal prospective ("and it was
never to be heard again") in which the clan has no existence. But
punishment is inflicted upon the Christians. The *egwugwu* destroy both Enoch's compound and the church, and Umuofia is
placated.
    When the district commissioner returns to Umuofia, however,
the six elders of Umuofia are imprisoned by a trick. After being
ridiculed by the court messengers, they are set free on the payment
of a fine and return home in disgrace to a subdued clan. Okonkwo
is infuriated by the treatment he has received and yet in a curious
way he is elated. "Before he had gone to bed he had brought down
his war dress, which he had not touched since his return from
exile. He had shaken out his smoked raffia skirt and examined his
full feather head-gear and his shield" (xxiv). This is the moment

he has been waiting for, a chance to redress the mysterious set-backs to his career, the frustration of the years of exile, the innumerable compromises. Now that his fears have been justified, the tribe must act. Looking back to his earlier successes, like the quarrel with Mbaino which opened the novel, Okonkwo hopes to recover his past authority by solving these new problems in the old way. But the old ways are no longer applicable, for the tribe is divided. Okonkwo and his friends seek to act with the old vigor and decision in this new situation: "If we fight the stranger we shall hit our brothers and perhaps shed the blood of a clansman. But we must do it. Our fathers never dreamt of such a thing, they never killed their brothers. But a white man never came to them. So we must do what our fathers would never have done. . . . We must root out this evil. And if our brothers take the side of evil we must root them out too" (xxiv). In their anxiety to force Umuofia into open conflict, Okonkwo's party use the extreme categories of their enemies. But Umuofia is not ready, and, as the court messengers appear, Okonkwo finds that the conflict is his alone. "In that brief moment the world seemed to stand still, waiting. There was utter silence. The men of Umuofia were merged into the mute back-cloth of trees and giant creepers, waiting" (xxiv). The head messenger orders the meeting to stop in the name of the white man. With two blows of his matchet Okonkwo beheads the man and knows immediately that the tribe will not support his action. "He knew that Umuofia would not go to war. He knew because they had let the other messenger escape. They had broken into tumult instead of action. He discerned fright in that tumult. He heard voices asking: 'Why did he do it?' " (xxiv).

He wipes his matchet on the sand and goes away to kill himself, thereby committing the final abomination, "an offence against the Earth, and a man who commits it will not be buried by his clansmen. His body is evil, and only strangers may touch it" (xxv). This is where Okonkwo's narrow rectitude has led him; the embodiment of traditional law has become the outcast of the tribe. The paradox prompts Obierika's final baffled cry to the D.C.: "That man was one of the greatest men in Umuofia. You drove him to kill himself; and now he will be buried like a dog . . ." (xxv). In his anguish, Obierika accuses the intruder of the death of his friend. But clearly, this is an oversimplification; the white man is the catalyst of a struggle which has been in progress since the beginning of the novel. At first, Okonkwo was dogmatically defending the letter of tribal law against the more humane members of the clan who insisted that this should be modified and controlled by its interplay with particular situations. With the arrival of the missionaries, Okonkwo's position became stronger; the flexibility and tolerance of Ibo society was shown to be the cause of its vulnerability. And so, just as at the beginning of the novel Okonkwo was successful in Umuofia because of his ignorance of its subtle dialectic, now he is its most stalwart defender because he is too obtuse to appreciate the attractions of the new religion. He himself has never been troubled by the discrepancy between the divine and human systems of value, and so a new reconciliation is of little interest. For a man who has consistently belittled sympathy and affection, a loving god is an irrelevance.

In his wrongheaded way he is correct in his resistance. Firm, decisive action at the outset might have repulsed the missionaries. As soon, however, as any kind of contact is permitted, then Achebe shows by the logic of his narrative that traditional tribal society is doomed. For this new religion questions radically all the basic tenets of Umuofia, and in providing answers to some of their dilemmas it undermines their other sanctities. Okonkwo acts as if he understands these dangers. He forces a clear-cut confrontation out of a complex process which has been going on for some time and seeks to involve against its will a society he does not understand in a war against the intruders. His isolation and suicide are inevitable, and they provide the final example of the dislocation between the human predicament and the divine decrees. Okonkwo will be buried like a dog in the "evil forest," rejected by the tribe and the Earth Mother he has defended with such loyalty.

As Okonkwo's life moves quickly to its tragic end, one is reminded forcibly of another impressive but wrongheaded hero, Henchard in *The Mayor of Casterbridge*. They share an obsessive need for success and status, they subordinate all their private relations to this end, and both have an inability to understand the tolerant, skeptical societies in which their novel single-mindedness succeeds. But the similarity becomes more striking when their worlds, threatened from the outside by disruptive forces, begin to disintegrate. Then, paradoxically, these aggressive and fiery individuals who achieved power by simplifying and finally flouting traditional values become the fierce defenders of the status quo,

and our sympathy shifts accordingly. Viewed in the perspective of
the Wessex, rustic way of life, Henchard is crass, brutal, and dangerous; but when this way of life as a whole is threatened with
imminent destruction, then his fierce resistance takes on a certain
grandeur. The reader's sympathy describes a similar trajectory as
it follows Okonkwo's career. By the values of Umuofia his inadequacies are very apparent; but when the alien religion begins to
question and undermine these values, Okonkwo, untroubled by
the heart-searching of the community, springs to its defense and
acts. But Umuofia, too disunited to follow his lead, capitulates to
the forces which will destroy it. Both men end their lives as outcasts, and their death is the price of the destructive compromises
which their communities are now forced to make. In this way,
Henchard and Okonkwo become for the only time in their lives
representative of a way of life which has been lost.

There is a final incident in the novel which reduces these
complexities to ironically manageable proportions. Supported by
his African soldiers who already speak colonial pidgin English,
the D.C. arrives on the scene to arrest Okonkwo. He finds that he
has hanged himself, and the tribe will not touch his abominated
body. As an amateur anthropologist his interest is immediately
kindled by this strange custom. The last page of the novel is presented from his point of view.

"Take down the body," the Commissioner ordered his chief messenger, "and bring it and all these people to the court."

"Yes, sah," the messenger said, saluting.

The Commissioner went away, taking three or four of the soldiers
with him. In the many years in which he had toiled to bring civilisation
to different parts of Africa he had learnt a number of things. One of
them was that a District Commissioner must never attend to such un-
dignified details as cutting down a hanged man from the tree. Such
attention would give the natives a poor opinion of him. In the book
which he planned to write he would stress that point. As he walked
back to the court he thought about that book. Every day brought him
some new material. The story of this man who had killed a messenger
and hanged himself would make interesting reading. One could almost
write a whole chapter on him. Perhaps not a whole chapter but a rea-
sonable paragraph, at any rate. There was so much else to include, and
one must be firm in cutting out details. He had already chosen the title
of the book, after much thought: *The Pacification of the Primitive
Tribes of the Lower Niger.* (xxv)

This is clearly the most radical shift of point of view in the whole novel. Our immersion in the world of Umuofia has continued up to the last page, and then Achebe has suddenly detached us from this sympathetically rendered world and asked us to share the point of view of the British D.C. who, from the outside, sees Umuofia as the world of primitive custom, the heart of darkness of the European imagination. The D.C. is not an unfamiliar figure; he comes at the end of a long line of explorers, missionaries, and administrators whose preconceptions have enabled them to find in Africa what they wished to find. Here he asks us to revoke the conventions and assumptions of the tribal world which Achebe has made us accept so effortlessly, and translate the tragic culmination of Okonkwo's career into the terms of colonial pacification and primitive customs, with which we are more familiar.

This ironical shift of perspective from the inside to the outside of the fictional world is a device whose function is clear. It reminds us that the assumptions we have come to accept in the course of the novel are not the only ones, indeed are not the usual ones, in that realm of experience we have been exploring. The device has been used most recently and effectively in William Golding's novels, and the comparison is instructive. One of his main purposes also is to reassess unexplored or stereotyped areas of experience; at the end of *Lord of the Flies*, when he shifts suddenly to the point of view of the captain, he is returning us to a conventional perspective whose familiar contours can never be the same again. Similarly in *The Inheritors*, the conventional is transformed into the alien, and the alien becomes the conventional. At the end of that novel, the neanderthal world whose reality we have shared is dramatically disturbed by the arrival of the mysterious creature, *homo sapiens*, already equipped one imagines with a stereotyped vision of his prehistoric predecessors. In each of these novels the author is recovering an area of experience from its stereotype, and the final ironic shift is to challenge the reader to apply the stereotype once more if he dare. The author is putting his fictional world to the test. What is undermined in *Things Fall Apart*, as in Golding's novels, is not the fictional world but the persistent, stubborn stereotype.

CHAPTER 3

No Longer at Ease

NO *Longer at Ease* (1960) is a tragicomic postscript to the moving events of Achebe's first novel. The central character is Obi Okonkwo, son of Nwoye and grandson of Okonkwo, and the action takes place in Nigeria in the 1950's, in a world which is the result of the intermingling of Europe and Africa whose original confrontation we witnessed in *Things Fall Apart*. In this world Achebe traces the decline of his hero from brilliant student to civil servant convicted of bribery and corruption. It reads like a postscript to the earlier novel because the same forces are at work but in a confused, diluted, and blurred form. Allegiances are not clearly defined, and attempts at redefinition are cynically abandoned. The forces of Christianity which officially superseded the old tribal ethic are themselves shown to be on the wane in the new generation, and no new creed appears likely to take their place. The downfall of the hero in this perplexing world is presented as neither tragic nor surprising.

The novel begins at the end of Obi's career, with his trial. The Judge of the High Court of Lagos in his summing up poses the question which the rest of the novel, a long retrospect of the hero's career, seeks to answer. "I cannot comprehend how a young man of your education and brilliant promise could have done this"(i). The judge's puzzlement is echoed by other Europeans. Only Green, Obi's immediate superior in the administration, has an explanation of his disgrace. He announces in the club, still a European enclave in these preindependence days, that "The African is corrupt through and through" because for centuries he "has been the victim of the worst climate in the world and of every imaginable disease. Hardly his fault. But he has been sapped mentally and physically"(i). This is why he remains decadent despite the benefits of Western education.

Then we switch to the point of view of Obi's fellow villagers.

The Lagos branch of the Umuofia Progressive Union is not interested at its emergency meeting in generalizations about endemic African corruption. They are more concerned with the details of the downfall of their favored son, whom they had sent to England to the university, who quickly got into debt, and who now requires the assistance of a lawyer. This is testing clan loyalty to the utmost. They too are baffled by Obi's conduct, but in their case it is his naïveté that troubles them. "He should not have accepted the money himself. What others do is tell you to go and hand it to their houseboy. Obi tried to do what everyone does without finding out how it was done"(i). However, they decide to stand by their precious investment since he is the only member of the clan in a European post, and their ancestors would not agree to his abandonment. "An only palm-fruit does not get lost in the fire."

This is how, in the first chapter, Achebe dramatizes diagrammatically the perplexity of the two cultures of which Obi is the hybrid product. To the Europeans it is inconceivable that someone who has had the privilege of a Western education should not adhere to the rules of conduct it enshrines. To the Africans of Umuofia it is disturbing that their most learned offspring, who has been educated for the glory of the clan and to look after their interests, should be so incompetent in the elementary conventions of bribe taking. At this point, the retrospect of Obi's career begins which brings us back finally full-circle to the present and the expressions of disbelief on the last page of the novel: "Everybody wondered why. The learned judge, as we have seen, could not comprehend how an educated young man and so on and so forth. The British Council man, even the men of Umuofia, did not know. And we must presume that, in spite of his certitude, Mr. Green did not know either" (xix). Within this frame of incomprehension and incredulity, Achebe seeks to show the logic of his hero's progress.

I   *The Journey Home*

The opening phase of Obi's career, presented in the first six chapters, covers the period from his departure for an English university to his return to Umuofia. It introduces us to the conflicts already present in his upbringing and those which have been added by his education in England; it sketches his first efforts to come to terms with the Nigeria he discovers on his return from abroad.

As in Achebe's first novel, the action proper begins with a tribal gathering. It is now two generations since Okonkwo's heyday, and the impressive ritual of the clan has been replaced by a Christian prayer meeting, conducted on this occasion by Nwoye (renamed Isaac), a retired Church of England catechist. This does not represent any clear-cut victory for the missionaries as we see when Mary, one of the most zealous of the Christian converts, pours out her extempore prayers. Out of the conflict of the earlier novel a curious amalgam has been formed:

"Oh God of Abraham, God of Isaac and God of Jacob," she burst forth, "the Beginning and the End. Without you we can do nothing. The great river is not big enough for you to wash your hands in. You have the yam and you have the knife; we cannot eat unless you cut us a piece. We are like ants in your sight. We are like little children who only wash their stomach when they bathe, leaving their back dry . . ." She went on and on reeling off proverb after proverb and painting picture after picture. (i)

The Christian gospel, preached in such an alien, aggressive way in *Things Fall Apart*, has been absorbed and Africanized in the intervening years, and this synthesis now represents the status quo.

For the moment, the synthesis appears stable and the people of Umuofia are launching Obi on the next stage of the dialectic, the quest for European education and the power this brings. And they want the genuine article, not simply the education brought by the missionaries, but a degree from an English university which gives access to a "European post" in the civil service. The attention of the clan has now shifted from religion to the new open-sesame, education, which is an invaluable asset in intervillage and intertribal rivalries. Even the Reverend Samuel Ikedi acknowledges this at the prayer meeting when he says that the departure of Obi is the fulfilment of the prophecy:

> The people which sat in darkness
> Saw a great light,
> And to them which sat in the region and shadow of death
> To them did light spring up. (i)

These are the words which made such a profound impression upon Obi's father during his perplexed childhood in the previous novel; but then the light was the new religion, now it is the new education. The struggle has shifted from the divine to the secular, but the Umuofians are employing the old terms to describe the new antinomies.

Mr. Ikedi does his best to contain this new development within religious terms: "In times past, Umuofia would have required of you to fight in her wars and bring home human heads. But those were days of darkness from which we have been delivered by the blood of the Lamb of God. Today we send you to bring knowledge. Remember that the fear of the Lord is the beginning of wisdom" (i). The attempted containment is by its nature doomed to failure. The Umuofians with characteristic flexibility appreciate the need for modern knowledge in order to defend and extend the gains already secured by their Christian compromise. This is why they want Obi to read law in England, "so that when he returned he would handle all their land cases against their neighbours" (i). But what they don't anticipate is that the knowledge which brings power also brings detachment and alienation, and that Obi's education far from simply being a weapon to defend the status quo—the establishment of which his grandfather died trying to prevent—is the next foray of the dialectical process. The old synthesis has, without their knowledge, become the new thesis which will in turn be questioned by the new values Obi brings back from abroad.

We can see that the alignment of forces no longer has the classical simplicity of earlier days. When Obi returns from England and the university, he comes, not to the village, but first to the Afro-European city of Lagos. This is to remind us that the clearly defined conflict between Africa and Europe is a thing of the past. The city stands midway between Europe and Umuofia and creates its own highly spiced amalgamation of their different cultural ingredients.

Obi's changing attitude to the city is a means of indicating his role in the dialectic described. His reactions are given schematically, in rapid succession. First, as a young member of the village community, he accepts the romantic accounts of this place, the nearest thing to Europe, where "There is no darkness . . . because at night the electric shines like the sun" (ii). Then on his way to England he spends a few days in the city with his friend. On this occasion, Obi "did not really see much of Lagos then. His mind was, as it were, on higher things" (ii), but what he does notice strikes him as sleazy and tawdry. Finally, on his return, the disillusionment is complete. Lagos is now a scenario of dead dogs, bad smells, and sewage.

Here was Lagos, thought Obi, the real Lagos he hadn't imagined existed until now. During his first winter in England he had written a callow, nostalgic poem about Nigeria. It wasn't Lagos in particular, but Lagos was part of the Nigeria he had in mind.

> "How sweet it is to lie beneath a tree
> At eventime and share the ecstacy
> Of jocund birds and flimsy butterflies;
> How sweet to leave our earthbound body in its mud,
> And rise towards the music of the spheres,
> Descending softly with the wind,
> And the tender glow of the fading sun."

He recalled this poem and then turned and looked at the rotting dog in the storm drain and smiled. "I have tasted putrid flesh in the spoon," he said through clenched teeth. "Far more apt." At last Clara emerged from the side street and they drove away. (ii)

Lagos, of course, has remained the same. What has changed so drastically is Obi and the stereotypes he seeks to impose on the city.

In *Things Fall Apart,* we had a glimpse of these stereotypes in their rudimentary form; we saw the white men with no toes through the eyes of the Umuofians and the primitive tribes of the lower Niger through the eyes of the district commissioner. Now, however, these images are in conflict within Obi's mind as he moves from Africa to England and back again. Thanks to his degree in English literature (he refused to read law), he is equipped to articulate the conflict: at one extreme, in his absence, Nigeria is translated into the terms of English pastoral; at the other extreme, on his return, it becomes the decaying waste land of the twentieth century. The violence of this change from one alien literary convention to another, although it is due in part to the rather cursory and diagrammatic treatment, manages to suggest the instability of the hybrid hero searching in vain for a stable point of view. As he

now drives home to his apartment in what was once the European
reserve of Ikoyi he muses on the "two cities in one," the symbol of
his own division: "It always reminded him of twin kernels
separated by a thin wall in a palm-nut shell. Sometimes one kernel
was shiny-black and alive, the other powdery-white and dead"
(ii). Although the analogy is reassuringly African, Obi is driving
to his European apartment, the perquisite of his European post.

The full extent of Obi's alienation only becomes apparent to the
members of the Umuofia Progressive Union at the reception it
holds in Lagos to celebrate his return from England. They have
paid to educate him and they expect a transformation. They
would, no doubt, find wholly admirable the conduct of Obi's fellow traveler who "as soon as Lagos had been sighted had returned
to his cabin to emerge half an hour later in a black suit, bowler
hat and rolled umbrella, even though it was a hot October day"
(iv). Unfortunately, Obi is one of the new wave of "been-tos," the
sophisticated avant-garde who express their independence by re-
verting defiantly to a few selected African customs. "The second
generation of educated Nigerians had gone back to eating
pounded yams or *garri* with their fingers for the good reason that
it tasted better that way. Also for the even better reason that they
were not as scared as the first generation of being called uncivil-
ised" (ii). Such conduct doesn't fit in with the preconceptions of
the Umuofians in Lagos. They are disturbed by Obi's appearance
(he turns up at the reception in shirtsleeves because of the heat),
by his unimpressive speech of thanks ("He spoke 'is' and 'was'"),
and by his strange system of values ("Education for service, not
for white-collar jobs and comfortable salaries"). The secretary in
his welcome address, which rigorously eschews "is" and "was,"
seeks to regain control of this child of Umuofia who has developed
peculiar habits. He reminds Obi that he has been sent to the university by the union and that they now expect to enjoy "the great
honour Obi had brought to the ancient town of Umuofia which
could now join the comity of other towns in their march towards
political irrendentism, social equality and economic emancipation." Or, in more direct terms, he is "an invaluable possession,"
"an investment which must yield heavy dividends" (iv). The
union's only concern is tribal solidarity and self-interest, and the
meeting ends rather uneasily with a discussion of bribery and in-

fluence, a subject which is to play an increasingly major part in the novel as the pressures begin to build up around the hero.

The disillusionment between Obi and the clan is mutual. He quickly feels that the demands being made upon him are unacceptable, that he is an alien with a different set of values. Again, it is bribery which drives this home. At his civil service interview the African member of the board asks only one question: "Why do you want a job in the Civil Service? So that you can take bribes?" (v). Then as he travels home on his first visit to the village, he witnesses the driver of his mammy-wagon bribing the police. Bribery has filtered down into the texture of daily life and is accepted as inevitable; the mammy-wagon carries the motto, "God's Case No Appeal."

This is the moment of Obi's extreme revulsion against his own country. He is a black Englishman whose knowledge of Africa only enables him to discern more clearly the precise nature of its corruption. He expresses his distaste in grandiloquent, almost colonial language:

"What an Augean stable!" he muttered to himself. "Where does one begin? With the masses? Educate the masses?" He shook his head. "Not a chance there. It would take centuries. A handful of men at the top. Or even one man with vision—an enlightened dictator. People are scared of the word nowadays. But what kind of democracy can exist side by side with so much corruption and ignorance? Perhaps a halfway house—a sort of compromise." (v)

Alienated from his own society, he assumes that reform will have to be imposed from outside. Obi sounds like a colonial describing the natives, and, as the next sentence indicates, he has even cultivated the expatriate's self-deprecatory gloss: "When Obi's reasoning reached this point he reminded himself that England had been as corrupt not so very long ago." The assumption is, of course, that Africa is evolving in the direction of Europe.

But Obi is also an African, and on the long journey home we see him moving along the whole spectrum of attitudes, from white critic to black son. Such a change begins during the night as he drowses in the cab of the mammy-wagon. Abandoning his attempt at "consecutive reasoning" about the condition of Nigeria, he dreams erotically of his girl friend Clara:

He said words in his mind that he could not say out aloud even when
he was alone. Strangely enough, all the words were in his mother
tongue. He could say any English word, no matter how dirty, but some
Ibo words simply would not proceed from his mouth. It was no doubt
his early training that operated this censorship, English words filtering
through because they were learnt later in life. (v)

This linguistic shift indicates the different levels of Obi's mind and
questions his earlier detached condemnation. The point is driven
home as he listens to the traders singing one of the songs he has
heard so many times before. He tries to translate the refrain,
which consists of five apparently unrelated sentences, into English. For the first time the meaning becomes clear: "On the face of
it there was no kind of logic or meaning in the song. But as Obi
turned it round and round in his mind, he was struck by the
wealth of association that even such a mediocre song could have."
As he explains its symbolic language we see that this is an Ibo
alternative to the "consecutive reasoning" he had rejected earlier.
Obi has switched from one mental process to another, from English to Ibo, and from literary cliché to Ibo folk song. In an incident of this kind, the two levels of Obi's mind communicate with
each other and he comes to understand the "meaning" of the
song when it is translated into the logical terms of English. Ironically, the theme of the song turns out to be the same as that of his
colonialist mutterings—"the world turned upside down."
    The novelist is probing his hero's inner tensions in this way as
he approaches Umuofia to complete the circle which began in the
first chapter with the farewell party. His reception by the villagers
is far more triumphant than the welcome by the critical Umuofians of Lagos. The village welcomes him as a returning hero,
without any suspicion of his cultural dislocation. For them he is
not only an Umuofian but also a son of their particular village,
Iguedo, and a key factor in intervillage rivalry. They greet him in
the same terms with which they dispatched him to England; he is
a modern successor of the great warriors Okonkwo, Ezeudu, and
Obierika.

These men were great in their day. Today greatness has changed its
tune. Titles are no longer great, neither are barns or large numbers of
wives and children. Greatness is now in the things of the white man.
And so we too have changed our tune. We are the first in all the nine

villages to send our son to the white man's land. Greatness has belonged to Iguedo from ancient times. It is not made by man. . . . The great tree chooses where to grow and we find it there, so it is with the greatness in men. (v)

But this apparently uncomplicated delight in Obi's success quickly breaks down into bickering and argument. Village life, which at the beginning of the novel seemed to be a stable synthesis of Ibo and Christian elements, now reveals itself to be a smoldering conflict which occasionally bursts into flame. Obi's return provides such an occasion.

The question at issue is, who is to gain the credit for Obi's triumph, the clan or the religion? He was sent off to England by the Reverend Samuel Ikedi as a new missionary fulfilling prophecy by bringing the light of education to the people which sat in darkness. Money was subscribed, however, by the whole of Umuofia, and so the elders feel justified in translating his success into their own tribal terms. Carried away by their nostalgia for Iguedo's days of glory, they praise him in the formulae of ancestor worship and have to be corrected by Obi's father:

"I am happy that you returned home safe," said Matthew to Obi.

"He is a son of Iguedo," said old Odogwu. "There are nine villages in Umuofia, but Iguedo is Iguedo. We have our faults, but we are not empty men who become white when they see white, and black when they see black."

Obi's heart glowed with pride within him.

"He is the grandson of Ogbuefi Okonkwo who faced the white man single-handed and died in the fight. Stand up!"

Obi stood up obediently.

"Remark him," said Odogwu. "He is Ogbuefi Okonkwo come back. He is Okonkwo *kpom-kwem*, exact, perfect."

Obi's father cleared his throat in embarrassment. "Dead men do not come back," he said.

"I tell you this is Okonkwo. As it was in the beginning so it will be in the end. That is what your religion tells us."

"It does not tell you that dead men return." (v)

The confrontation of *Things Fall Apart* has been reduced to this kind of squabble. And it has begun even before Obi's arrival. The lavish celebrations that have been organized are jeopardized by rain, and yet Obi's father, stubbornly doctrinaire, won't take the logical precaution. "In fact, many people half wished it would rain heavily so as to show Isaac Okonkwo that Christianity had made him blind. He was the only man who failed to see that on an occasion such as this he should take palm-wine, a cock and a little money to the chief rain-maker in Umuofia" (v). Isaac's recalcitrance in conflict with the sentimental nostalgia of the old men of the village dramatizes with controlled irony the continuing tensions in Umuofia. It is noticeable that Achebe crystallizes these tensions far more confidently in this kind of discussion than in the psychological analysis of Obi's schizophrenia.

The old men return to the attack and insist that, since Obi has returned from the land of the spirits, kola nut must be broken in thanks. Isaac, the Christian censor, is watching carefully:

"This is a Christian house," replied Obi's father.
"A Christian house where kola nut is not eaten?" sneered the man.
"Kola nut is eaten here," replied Mr. Okonkwo, "but not sacrificed to idols."
"Who talked about sacrifice? Here is a little child returned from wrestling in the spirit world and you sit there blabbing about Christian house and idols, talking like a man whose palm-wine has gone into his nose."

For the moment a reconciliation is effected. Obi shows the kola nut round and then presents it to Odogwu, a witty and unrepentant pagan who "went to church once a year at harvest" and "knew one or two things about Christianity." It is he who, with the old Ibo flexibility and savoir faire, manages to bypass the imminent collision:

He took the saucer, drew up his knees together to form a table and placed the saucer there. He raised his two hands, palms facing upwards, and said: "Bless this kola nut so that when we eat it it will be good in our body in the name of Jesu Kristi. As it was in the beginning it will be at the end. Amen." Everyone replied Amen and cheered old Odogwu on his performance. Even Okonkwo could not help joining in the cheers.
"You should become a Christian," he suggested.
"Yes, if you will agree to make me a pastor," said Odogwu.
Everyone laughed again. (v)

This is a reminder of the old Ibo confidence and wit, and Achebe's style regains its tautness when he dramatizes these astringent exchanges. The aplomb of Odogwu as he manipulates the two cultures is a sad comment on Obi's passivity.

The crisis of Obi's return indicates clearly that however thoroughly the Ibo and Christian ingredients are mixed they will never coalesce. On the slightest pretext they separate and regroup for open conflict. What appeared earlier to be a genuinely dialectical process is seen under Achebe's scrutiny to be no such thing. As Obi retraces the stages of the outward journey which took him from Iguedo to Lagos, and then to England, we witness the several cultural rapprochements disintegrating under the conflicts which his return reawakens. The U.P.U. in Lagos reverted to simple tribal self-interest when it suspected Obi of jettisoning his Umuofian affiliations. Similarly, here in the village, all the elements in the conflict which began with the arrival of the missionaries, are quickly disengaged from their temporary synthesis and thrown into the flux again. And now there is an additional ingredient. Obi has returned with a fastidious self-consciousness which rejects both the narrow self-interest of the clan and the simplicities of his father's naïve faith.

The return journey into increasing uncertainty ends at his parents' home, and here too at the deepest layer of his past Obi discovers an unresolved conflict. His parents have always stressed different aspects of the hybrid village culture in the upbringing of their children. His father, as village catechist, insisted dogmatically upon the Christian nature of their education, while his mother tried to modify this quietly but insistently with her native folklore. "She was a very devout woman, but Obi used to wonder whether, left to herself, she would not have preferred telling her children the folk-stories that her mother had told her" (vi). Obi remembers how as a child the two sides of this double heritage frustrated each other: he both mistranslated his Bible lessons and was unable to narrate folk stories at school. Although he and his brothers and sisters lived in the village, they did not belong to it. They were not allowed to accept food in neighbors' houses because there food was offered to idols. "That fact alone set her children apart from all others for, among the Ibo, children were free to eat where they liked" (vi). So here, in Obi's early child-

hood, we find division and alienation; again an apparent reconciliation masks very real differences. And even in their old age his
parents persist in their old allegiances as stubbornly as ever; his
father has to be reassured about Obi's (nonexistent) Christian
faith, while his mother's world is still inhabited by *chis* and un-
friendly spirits.

As Obi composes himself for sleep in his parents' house with the
familiar sound of rain on the roof, it is clear that the first phase of
the novel has ended. It began with Achebe quickly sketching the
stages of his hero's outward journey to England and the change of
values each necessitated. Then came the return movement which
cynically dismantled the dialectic which had been carefully built
up. At each stage of his return, Obi awakens into life the latent
antagonisms, the unresolved antinomies upon which his outward
progress had apparently been securely built. Each synthesis turns
out to have been merely a temporary truce between different values and cultures. When he has learned this sobering lesson Obi is
ready to begin his civil service career in Lagos.

II *Lagos*

For the rest of the novel the hero lives and works in Lagos and
it is here, where Africa and Europe meet most dramatically, that
the contradictions of his background are translated into action.
They center upon two main issues—duty and marriage. In his
vacillating attitude to these Obi reveals the full extent of the deep
division in his nature.

At first, the stress is upon duty in one's profession. An extreme
version is represented by Mr. Green, Obi's immediate superior.
He sees the pursuit of duty as an end in itself, quite divorced from
personal interest of any kind. This gives it a kind of purity, which
Obi admires, but also an impersonality which is disconcerting:

Obi had long come to admit to himself that, no matter how much he
disliked Mr. Green, he nevertheless had some admirable qualities.
Take, for instance, his devotion to duty. Rain or shine, he was in the
office half an hour before the official time, and quite often worked
long after two, or returned again in the evening. Obi could not understand it. Here was a man who did not believe in a country, and yet
worked so hard for it. Did he simply believe in duty as a logical
necessity? . . . He was like a man who had some great and supreme
task that must be completed before a final catastrophe intervened. (xi)

The catastrophe in his case would be Nigeria's political independence for this would destroy overnight the stereoype of Africa his duty is serving. Such an event would create new and complex responsibilities that he is incapable of fulfilling.

Obi, the incipient novelist ("I must write a novel on the tragedy of the Greens of this century"), analyzes with amused detachment his superior's dilemma:

It was clear he loved Africa, but only Africa of a kind: the Africa of Charles, the messenger, the Africa of his garden-boy and steward-boy. He must have come originally with an ideal—to bring a light to the heart of darkness, to tribal head-hunters performing weird ceremonies and unspeakable rites. But when he arrived, Africa played him false. Where was his beloved bush full of human sacrifice? There was St. George horsed and caparisoned, but where was the dragon? In 1900 Mr. Green might have ranked among the great missionaries; in 1935 he would have made do with slapping headmasters in the presence of their pupils; but in 1957 he could only curse and swear. (xi)

Green's ideal of duty has become increasingly divorced from the situation in which he exercises it; the more rigorously and puritanically he enforces it, the more intensely he comes to hate the Africans who do not conform to its premise. Here we see Achebe beginning to explore in more detail the stereotypes imposed by Europe upon Africa. The glimpse we had into the mind of the British district commissioner in *Things Fall Apart* is developed into the character of Green, and will in Achebe's next novel culminate in his major expatriate character, Winterbottom. As the author explores this discrepancy between an ideal of duty and the situation where it is to be applied, he acknowledges his debt to Conrad:

With a flash of insight Obi remembered his Conrad which he had read for his degree. "By the simple exercise of our will we can exert a power for good practically unbounded." That was Mr. Kurtz before the heart of darkness got him. Afterwards he had written: "Exterminate all the brutes." It was not a close analogy, of course. Kurtz had succumbed to the darkness, Green to the incipient dawn. But their beginning and their end were alike. (xi)

As the discrepancy widens and the situation fails to measure up to the ideal, there is a sense in which the ideal thereby becomes more secure and inviolate. It cannot now be compromised by reality.

This is one extreme. At the other, we have duty and loyalty as envisaged by the U.P.U. There is nothing abstract or preconceived about their views; their ethic is empirical and situational, and it is based upon the solidarity and continuance of the tribe. Fellow Umuofians in Lagos help one another because it is to everyone's mutual advantage. That this tribal ethic is still strong is immediately apparent from the first meeting of the U.P.U. which Obi attends after settling in Lagos. As he gets out of his new car he is greeted with the traditional formula:

> "*Umuofia kwenu!*" shouted one old man.
> "Ya!" replied everyone in unison.
> "*Umuofia kwenu!*"
> "Ya!"
> "*Kwenu!*"
> "Ya!"

The meeting quickly gets down to business, and we see the meaning of tribalism in twentieth-century Lagos. It is a mutual protection society for procuring jobs and promotion by means of influence and bribes. This is why the U.P.U. is so delighted by Obi's return. Having invested in his career at great sacrifice, they now look forward to the rewards, and it is Obi's duty to make these as ample as possible. As one old man says:

> "That is why we say that he who has people is richer than he who has money. Everyone of us here should look out for openings in his department and put in a word for Joshua." This was greeted with approval.
> "Thanks to the Man Above," he continued, "we now have one of our sons in the senior service. We are not going to ask him to bring his salary to share among us. It is in little things like this that he can help us. It is our fault if we do not approach him. Shall we kill a snake and carry it in our hand when we have a bag for putting long things in." (viii)

One uses one's profession to help fellow Umuofians and so pay back one's debt to the tribe. Like Green's very different concept of duty this can be looked at in two ways. From one point of view it is an impressive continuation into the modern city of the communal solidarity we witnessed in its traditional form at the turn of the century. As Obi says in his carefully rehearsed speech of thanks: "Our fathers have a saying about the danger of living apart. They say it is the curse of the snake. If all snakes lived together in one place, who would approach them? But they live every one unto himself and so fall easy prey to man" (viii). By the side of this, Green's professional diligence and rectitude seem bleak and inhuman. And yet, from another point of view, tribal solidarity when transferred from the country to the town becomes nepotism and self-interest. If one is continually in debt to one's community, one must acknowledge this and yet pretend to act as an independent agent. The ambiguity of this relationship soon becomes apparent to Obi when he asks if he may delay the repayment of his loan. The union agrees to his request, but the President takes the opportunity to give Obi some advice on how to manage his finances, and he ends: "You may ask why I am saying all this. I have heard that you are moving around with a girl of doubtful ancestry, and even thinking of marrying her. . . ." To their amazement, Obi storms out in a rage at this attempt to interfere in his private affairs.

Behind these two versions of duty lie contradictory views of the individual in society. In the more atomistic view, the individual is solitary and self-sufficient; the course of duty he follows is a means of exercising his will and testing his integrity. The organic view, on the other hand, stresses that the individual is a member of a community and all his actions are controlled by this fact. Duty is the constant awareness of the self as an integral part of the organic whole of the village or tribe through which one acts and achieves identity. European individualism and African tribalism—expressed in these terms it becomes parody—meet in the confused no man's land of the city which misrepresents both. The former becomes embittered alienation, the latter blatant nepotism. Mannoni, no doubt, would say that both the colonial and the colonized get what they deserve. Obi, unfortunately, is in the position of sympathizing with both parties. He has been educated at great cost by his clan, but the lesson he has learned best is the inviolable independence of the individual.

At first, Obi is confident he can balance both sets of claims. He explains neatly to his friend Christopher that bribery in public life is restricted to earlier generations of civil servants: "Take one of these old men. He probably left school thirty years ago in Standard Six. He has worked steadily to the top through bribery—an ordeal by bribery. To him the bribe is natural. He gave it and he expects it. Our people say that if you pay homage to the man on top, others will pay homage to you when it is your turn to be on top." Young men, on the other hand, now gain promotion without bribing anyone: "It's not that they're necessarily better than others, it's simply that they can afford to be virtuous" (ii). It is only a question of paying back his loan to the U.P.U. and then he can live his own life. But as the various periodical payments of a government official fall due—income tax, electricity, car—Obi becomes more and more dependent upon the good will of Umofia at the same time as he is stoutly resisting their interference in his private affairs. Despite his difficulties he firmly resists the first offer of a bribe to procure a federal scholarship. The candidate's brother offers money, the candidate offers herself, but Obi is firm and feels he has won his first victory in the battle against corruption. He is not even deflated by Christopher's subsequent skepticism—the girl obtained a scholarship anyway, probably by bribing the other members of the board.

We notice, however, that Obi doesn't manage his balancing act with anything like the facility of his friend Christopher or the Hon. Sam Okoli. The latter, an early version of Chief Nanga, plays with his European tape-recorders and is full of praise for the deferential efficiency of his secretary, an Oxford man; but he always remembers to redress the balance. "I respect the white man although we want them to go." Or more effectively in pidgin English: "This no be them country" (vii). Obi is too deeply committed to both sides to manipulate them in this calculating manner.

What finally makes a reconciliation impossible is Obi's chronic shortage of money. He is unable to fulfill his obligations and at the same time live the life expected of a civil servant in a European post. In order to ease his conscience over this failure he is forced to resort to the kind of dualism which was such a pervasive feature of Ibo life in *Things Fall Apart*. The people of Umuofia must realize, he says, that he is *both* a member of their community and a civil servant and that the two roles are quite separate.

What [his people] did not know was that, having laboured in sweat and tears to enrol their kinsman among the shining élite, they had to

keep him there. Having made him a member of an exclusive club
whose members greet one another with "How's the car behaving?" did
they expect him to turn round and answer: "I'm sorry, but my car is
off the road. You see I couldn't pay my insurance premium?" That
would be letting the side down in a way that was quite unthinkable.
Almost as unthinkable as a masked spirit in the Ibo society answering
another's esoteric salutation: "I'm sorry, my friend, but I don't understand your strange language. I'm but a human being wearing a mask."
No, these things could not be. (x)

This is a regression from his earlier attempt to reconcile conflicting
claims. The final stage is a compromise by which Obi halfheartedly and ineffectively conforms to neither set of values: he accepts
some bribes but refuses to consider anyone for a scholarship who
does not possess the minimum academic qualifications.

The regression from his earlier ideals has been quickened by
the problems which bedevil his private life. Here again Obi finds
himself trapped between two very different systems of value. On
the boat from England he has fallen in love with an Ibo girl,
Clara. For the first time he is ready to believe that romantic love
might be more than "another grossly overrated European inven-
tion." Previously, Obi had always remained detached and critical.
"There was always a part of him, the thinking part, which seemed
to stand outside it all watching the passionate embrace with cynical disdain. The result was that one half of Obi might kiss a girl
and murmur: 'I love you,' but the other half would say: 'Don't be
silly'" (vii). With Clara, however, it was different. Yet she shows
a curious reluctance to becoming involved with Obi. It is only
when they are back in Nigeria that she tells him the reason: she
can't marry him because she is an *osu*. Obi, flaunting his European
code of values, is outraged that anyone should feel themselves
tied by this traditional taboo: "It was scandalous that in the
middle of the twentieth century a man could be barred from marrying a girl simply because her great-great-great-great-grandfa-
ther had been dedicated to serve a god, thereby setting himself
apart and turning his descendants into a forbidden caste to the end
of Time" (vii). He insists they become engaged and, although
warned by his friend Joseph that his "mission-house upbringing
and European education had made him a stranger in his country,"
he feels confident that he can still live his own life.

Quickly the complications and pressures build up again. The

U.P.U. is appalled when it hears of his conduct and seeks to influence him through his financial dependence. Then his relations with Clara deteriorate as she becomes hysterically insistent that they break off the engagement. But Obi refuses stubbornly to be controlled by outdated tribal practices; he is an individual who must be allowed to exercise the supreme choice of his own wife. Finally, word gets back to the village, and Obi is summoned home by his father to meet the fiercest opposition of all.

As soon as Obi gets home, the claims of kinship begin to reassert themselves almost imperceptibly through the casual introduction of songs, tales, and proverbs. These, which were part of the accepted texture of traditional life in Umuofia, now nag persistently at the independence of the hero. A group of singers on the way home from a funeral remind Obi that

> He that has a brother must hold him to his heart,
> For a kinsman cannot be bought in the market,
> Neither is a brother bought with money. (xiii)

And his father hopes he has kept his Umuofian contacts in Lagos for "in a strange land one should always move near one's kinsmen" (xiv). What makes the impending quarrel more unwelcome is his mother's illness.

When at last he discloses whom he wants to marry, his father's reaction is unexpected: "His father laughed. It was the kind of laughter one sometimes heard from a masked ancestral spirit. He would salute you by name and ask you if you knew who he was. You would reply with one hand humbly touching the ground that you did not, that he was beyond human knowledge. Then he might laugh as if through a throat of metal. And the meaning of that laughter was clear: 'I did not really think you would know, you miserable human worm!'" Disconcertingly, we are back in the world of *Things Fall Apart*. When Obi argues with his father that they as Christians cannot accept the *osu* prohibition ("The Bible says that in Christ there are no bond or free"), the somber reply is:

Osu is like leprosy in the minds of our people. I beg of you, my son, not to bring the mark of shame and of leprosy into your family. If you do, your children and your children's children unto the third and fourth generations will curse your memory. It is not for myself I speak; my

days are few. You will bring sorrow on your head and on the heads of
your children. Who will marry your daughters? Whose daughters will
your sons marry? Think of that, my son. We are Christians, but we cannot marry our own daughters. (xiv)

In this argument Obi has abandoned his agnosticism and reverted
to his earlier Christianity, while his father has abandoned his decades of Christian belief and reverted to the tribal law of his childhood. "Obi used the very words that his father might have used in
talking to his heathen kinsmen." But we now recognize that this
reversal of roles is the characteristic movement of the novel. In
times of crisis this regression to earlier beliefs emphatically denies
any evolutionary assimilation of cultures which the framework of
events might suggest. Here, it undermines even further the shaky
structure of values sketched out in the first phase of the novel.
Then it did appear that the foundations at least were firm and
that Obi's parents embodied irrevocably the opposing yet rudimentary elements of his nature. This latest crisis shows that the
dismantling of the dialectic of values does not stop here. Isaac
Nwoye Okonkwo jettisons his hard-won Christian faith and in his
old age opposes his son's marriage not on the grounds of moral or
religious principles but from a deeper level of experience—a lifetime of isolation and suffering.

Refusing to quarrel with Obi, Isaac simply recounts in a low
monotone the central episode from his early life which was the
crux of Achebe's previous novel. "I was no more than a boy when
I left my father's house and went with the missionaries. He placed
a curse on me. I was not there but my brother told me it was true.
When a man curses his own child it is a terrible thing. And I was
his first son." The familiar story of the death of Ikemefuna is now
presented in the perspective of Isaac's life. It leads to the following conclusion:

I tell you all this so that you may know what it was in those days to
become a Christian. I left my father's house, and he placed a curse on
me. I went through fire to become a Christian. Because I suffered I
understand Christianity—more than you will ever do. (xiv)

This is why he can speak with the authority of a masked ancestral
spirit: he has entered a realm of experience which will always be
closed to his son. He uses his authority to dissuade Obi from mar-

rying an *osu*. It is a change of allegiance for which we have not
been prepared and yet it continues the basic strategy of questioning skeptically the values of the hero's background. The implication of this latest reversion is that the basic antimony of Christian
and tribal from which all the previous conflicts and tensions arose
is itself in the final resort a false antithesis. Beneath all innovation
and modification lies the indestructible and unrelenting solidarity
of the tribe.

The anticipated opposition from his mother simply underlines
this. Her horror at his proposed marriage can only be expressed
through the symbols of a dream: "I was lying on a bed spread
with white cloth and I felt something creepy against my skin. I
looked down on the bed and found that a swarm of white termites
had eaten it up, and the mat and the white cloth. Yes, termites
had eaten up the bed right under me" (xiv). Now she sees the
meaning of the dream. If Obi wants to marry an *osu*, he must wait
until his mother is dead. "But if you do the thing while I am alive,
you will have my blood on your head, because I shall kill myself."
This instinctual opposition of his mother is more disturbing even
than that of his father because it cannot be explained and discussed. She expresses through her dream the collective horror of
the tribe at the proposed act of sacrilege. Obi's unease which cen-
tered first on his professional ethics and then became more acute
with his engagement to Clara has now turned into utter despair.
Superficial compromises have been resolved into deep divisions,
and these in turn translated into basic familial and tribal instincts.
This has been for him a dismembering of the self, and now he has
no will with which to assert himself.

His mind was troubled not only by what had happened but also by the
discovery that there was nothing in him with which to challenge it
honestly. All day he had striven to rouse his anger and his conviction,
but he was honest enough with himself to realise that the response he
got, no matter how violent it sometimes appeared, was not genuine.
It came from the periphery, and not the centre, like the jerk in the leg
of a dead frog when a current is applied to it. (xiv)

He can neither accept his parents' values nor reject them. He is
not only a product of Umuofia, but also of Lagos and Europe, and
these are a part of his character. Sickened, he realizes that al-

though the ramshackle structure of his life has been dismantled he cannot return to its origin. Now more than ever is he no longer at ease here, in the old dispensation.

He returns to Lagos and Clara. As soon as she understands what has happened she breaks off the engagement. Obi's financial problems are again becoming critical when he learns that Clara is pregnant. He manages to find money for a bungled abortion which leaves her ill and embittered. Finally, he hears of his mother's death, and any lingering loyalties are dissipated. Obi's absence from the funeral is called "a thing of shame," and his conduct is equated with his father's rebellion against the clan. "A man may go to England," says the President of the U.P.U., "become a lawyer or a doctor, but it does not change his blood. It is like the bird that flies off the earth and lands on an ant-hill. It is still on the ground" (xviii). As far as Umuofia is concerned, everything can be reduced to this depressingly simple formula: all the conflicts and permutations of Obi's career have been caused by his disloyalty to the tribe. Their own loyalty is so unquestioning that now, despite their criticism, they come to sympathize with him on his mother's death, and since Ikoyi is a European reserve they tactfully refrain from singing hymns.

All that remains to Obi is the feeling of guilt at the way he has treated his mother. This too can be removed by one of the self-defensive tricks he has learned from his tribulations. He exchanges the accusing image of his mother for a more convenient one, that of "the woman who got things done." The story which gives significance to this switch is that of the sacred he-goat who became an annoyance at the mission where his parents worked early in their marriage. All their complaints to the priest of Udo were ignored until one day the goat made the mistake of entering his mother's kitchen and eating the precious yam she was about to cook: "She took a sharp matchet and hewed off the beast's head. There were angry threats from village elders. The women for a time refused to buy from her or sell to her in the market." By remembering his mother as a person who acted promptly and instinctively as the situation demanded Obi is able to eradicate the later reproachful image and, equally important, find support and justification for the new empiricism he has rescued from his disillusionment. Now, the memory of his mother seemed to release his spirit. He no longer felt guilt. He, too, had died. Beyond death there are no ideals and no humbug, only reality. The impatient idealist says: "Give me a place to stand and I shall move the earth." But such a place does not exist. We all have to stand on the earth itself and go with her at her pace. The most horrible sight in the world cannot put out the eye. (xix)

Since all other possibilities have been systematically destroyed by the events of the novel, he has turned his guilt and despair into a philosophy, a new realism. This is all that Obi can salvage from the rich double heritage of his upbringing and education, but for a moment it seems that he may be able to accommodate himself to life in Lagos. He is not allowed the final comfort of his cynical realism. His conscience demands to the bitter end that the bribes he accepts must not overrule the regulations too blatantly, and so his last compromise proves to be neither profitable nor honest. His apprehension by the police at the end is a release from a dilemma which has no end.

The novel ends, as it began, at the trial where Africans and Europeans alike are dismayed by this sudden débâcle of Obi's career. To the outsider everything appeared to be in the hero's favor; only the reader familiar with the intimate details of Obi's private life is able to understand the logic of his disgrace. Achebe is again using in a less radical form the ironic distancing device he employed so effectively in *Things Fall Apart*. But is the irony justified on this occasion? Can we supply with confidence the answers to the judge's baffled questions? As we have seen, the novel is an exercise in diagnosis. The first part diagrammatically sets out the various ingredients of Obi's background as he journeys from Umuofia to Europe and back again. We quickly realize that, despite first appearances, the ingredients remain quite separate and unsynthesized. This is corroborated when Obi settles in Lagos. There his career and Clara undermine even further the values which had briefly coalesced, and through increasing disillusionment he quickly reaches the cul de sac of his final, uneasy skepticism. The diagnosis is meticulously conducted but the central character never crystallizes out of these disparate fragments. His character is carefully built up and then dismantled before our eyes, but Obi himself remains shadowy.

Admittedly, this is part of the author's intention: Obi is an alien created out of a miscellany of cultural elements, and the scaffolding of his character is meant to be ramshackle. But it would be a fallacy to accept this as justification for the disturbing void at the center of the novel. The diagrams of forces, the exemplary episodes, the schematic journeys fail to conceal the absence of any graspable self of the main character. It is not simply that Obi's career is confused, muddled, and an anticlimax. Achebe is aware of the nature of his hero's tragedy and seeks to justify it at the civil service interview early in the novel. There, Obi theorizes glibly about the "happy ending" of Graham Greene's *The Heart of the Matter:*

Perhaps happy ending is too strong, but there is no other way I can put it. The police officer is torn between his love of a woman and his love of God, and he commits suicide. It's much too simple. Tragedy isn't like that at all. I remember an old man in my village, a Christian convert, who suffered one calamity after another. He said life was like a bowl of wormwood which one sips a little at a time world without end. He understood the nature of tragedy. (v)

But even if we agree with him that "real tragedy is never resolved. It goes on hopelessly for ever," we still need at the center of the action an individual we may not only understand but sympathize with. This is especially true of the tragedy of the everyday where the anguish lies in each subtle response to the prosaic and the frequent. No such individual emerges from Obi's relations with his parents—they are simply the two components of his childhood world—nor with Clara—their relationship is conveyed in threadbare romantic cliché. Obi is a thoroughly passive character compelled to act occasionally by the exigencies of his various dilemmas. It might be argued that these dilemmas which arise from his inner contradictions represent Obi's character. But surely this is too deterministic a view. As several of Achebe's minor characters show, no one is simply the result of a cultural and hereditary dialectic. But this is what the author seems to believe with regard to his hero. When he has carried out the construction and dismantling of Obi's character there is nothing left, no carryover from the conflict and alliance of forces to the self of the hero which is their real battleground.

The method of narration should have been a decisive factor here. The events of the novel, apart from the framework of the trial, are described in the third person from the point of view of the hero. However, we never get any impression of a mind—even an alienated, deracinated mind—trying to impose a pattern of meaning upon the events of the novel. Through Obi's eyes we watch the incidents unfold and wonder what their relevance is to the standpoint from which they are described. At the end, when the questions are asked in court, we are aware of the cultural and social forces in conflict in the life of the typically educated Ibo villager, but we do not know why Obi Okonkwo has been determined and destroyed by them in the way that he has. And it is this absence of particularity which, according to the paradoxical logic of fiction, limits in a drastic way the general significance of the hero's career and the novel as a whole. Because he does not come alive as a unique individual, we are never encouraged to see in his predicament the more universal theme it implies. Misunderstanding between generations and cultural dislocation are not limited to any one country. But the significance of Achebe's second novel, unlike his first, does not reverberate beyond its regional setting. It remains, in a limiting sense, a West African novel.

CHAPTER 4

Arrow of God

I *The Priest of Ulu*

IN his third novel, *Arrow of God* (1964), Achebe goes back to Ibo village life in the 1920's before it has experienced any sustained contact with Europeans. The white man has arrived and is administering the country, but remotely from his hill station in a neighboring district. The significant change from *Things Fall Apart*, the events of which occurred a few years previously, is that the villagers realize they must come to terms with this alien rule which is both powerful and permanent. The author has chosen as his central character the aged Ezeulu who, as his name indicates, is the Chief Priest of Ulu, the most powerful of all the deities of the six villages of Umuaro. Ezeulu's role is to interpret to Umuaro the will of the god and to perform the two most important rituals in the life of the villages—the festival of the Pumpkin Leaves and that of the New Yam.

The first of these ceremonies cleanses the six villages of their sins before the planting season. The great decorated Ikolo drum, fashioned from a giant iroko tree "as old as Ulu himself at whose order the tree was cut down and its trunk hollowed out" (vii), greets the six villages in their ancient order, salutes Ulu, and finally summons Ezeulu from the shrine of the god. We see that Achebe has lost none of his skill in capturing the tension of communal Ibo rituals, with their strange mingling of fear and delight.

He wore smoked raffia which descended from his waist to the knee. The left half of his body—from forehead to toes—was painted with white chalk. Around his head was a leather band from which an eagle's feather pointed backwards. On his right hand he carried *Nne Ofo*, the mother of all staffs of authority in Umuaro, and in his left he held a long iron staff which kept up a quivering rattle whenever he struck its pointed end into the earth. He took a few long strides, pausing on each foot. Then he ran forward again as though he had seen a comrade in the vacant air; he stretched his arm and waved his staff to the right

and to the left. And those who were near enough heard the knocking
together of Ezeulu's staff and another which no one saw. At this many
fled in terror before the priest and the unseen presences around him.
(vii)

Half black, half white, Ezeulu is the intermediary between the
human world and the spirit world. As the narrator's impersonal
description changes to the frightened view of a villager, the man
in raffia is transformed into the divine intermediary inhabiting his
mysterious world.

Ezeulu then re-enacts the first coming of Ulu in the distant past
when the six villages sought help against the soldiers of Abam
who came to burn their houses and carry off their people into
slavery. Powerful medicine men created a common deity named
Ulu, whose priest became the Chief Priest of Umuaro. From that
day they were never defeated by an enemy in battle. Ezeulu cel-
brates this event and then performs the ceremony of purification.
As he runs round the marketplace the women throw their bunches
of pumpkin leaves and implore him to exorcize the sins of their
households. The priest runs into his shrine, and the tension is re-
leased: "The crowd seemed to rouse itself quickly to the knowledge that their Chief Priest was safe in his shrine, triumphant over
the sins of Umuaro which he was now burying deep into the earth
with the six bunches of leaves" (vii). Finally, the women dance,
each village in turn, and a vast cloud of dust rises from their feet
as they stamp in unison, pounding and smashing the pumpkin
leaves strewn thickly about the marketplace.

The second major ceremony, the feast of the New Yam, sancti-
fies the harvest and so marks the end of the old year and the
beginning of the new. On this occasion, every grown man in
Umuaro takes a seed-yam to the shrine of Ulu, and from these the
elders can reckon the number of men in each village. From these
Ezeulu also selects thirteen to calculate the new year. Only when
these have been ritually eaten can the festival take place and the
harvesting begin. As the novel opens, Ezeulu is peering up into
the sky looking for the new moon. Despite his age, he refuses to
believe his sight is deteriorating or that he is in any way inferior to
the young men of the villages who are not what they used to be in
his youth: "There was one game Ezeulu was never tired of playing on them. Whenever they shook hands with him he tensed his
arm and put all his power into the grip, and being unprepared for

it they winced and recoiled with pain" (i). At last, he sees the moon "as thin as an orphan fed grudgingly by a cruel foster-mother," and with the customary fear mingled with the joy of his high office he beats the iron gong. Then, while the villagers are welcoming the moon, he selects one of the sacred yams from his barn, roasts and eats it. Finally, he thanks Ulu for allowing him to see another new moon and begs good fortune for the six villages: "May children put their fathers into the earth and not fathers their children. . . . May good come to the land of the riverain folk and to the land of the forest peoples" (i).

By means of these two festivals Ezeulu controls both planting and harvesting, and the village year which is dependent upon them. And yet, as he carries out his yam ritual, the Chief Priest is perplexed and uncertain. He has begun to question the crucial role he plays in the life of the six villages. What kind of power does he really wield? "It was true he named the day for the feast of the Pumpkin Leaves and for the New Yam feast; but he did not choose the day. He was merely a watchman." Perhaps his power is illusory, and he is simply the passive intermediary between the god and the villages. Ezeulu's pride will not allow self-doubt of this kind: "No! the Chief Priest of Ulu was more than that, must be more than that. If he should refuse to name the day there would be no festival—no planting and no reaping." But the questions persist—"could he refuse? No Chief Priest had ever refused. So it could not be done. He would not dare." Then again comes the angry riposte: "No man in all Umuaro can stand up and say that I dare not." But the inner debate has not removed his misgivings: "His mind still persisted in trying to look too closely at the nature of his power. What kind of power was it if everybody knew that it would never be used?" (i). As his ceremonial appearance indicates, Ezeulu is half man, half spirit; in the world of man he is very powerful, in the world of spirits he is a servant. What is the true relationship between his two roles? Where does his primary duty lie, with the god or the tribe? These are some of the questions the events of the novel will seek to answer.

Some of the same questions, we remember, were being asked in Umuofia as the events of *Things Fall Apart* began to move toward their tragic climax and the discrepancy between human and divine values became more and more apparent. In *Arrow of God* Achebe focuses immediately on this problem of conflicting values

and roles and chooses as his central character someone who embodies this dilemma in its most acute form—the Chief Priest of
Ulu who is also a proud, opinionated, and domineering old man.
Like Okonkwo, he is convinced that he must obey to the letter the
commands of the god; unlike Okonkwo, he alone is equipped to
translate these commands to the tribe. In this situation, Ezeulu is
constantly tempted to mingle his own wishes with those of the
god and then assert his authority over the six villages by means of
Ulu's oracular power. But as Okonkwo found, a society based on a
flexible balancing of competing claims is not the most comfortable
place for a domineering personality. No one, not even a god, is
safe from criticism; there are always other people, other gods,
ready to supplant their predecessors in these shifting, skeptical
Ibo communities.

Ezeulu is conscious of his vulnerable position and this is why he
is scrutinizing so closely the nature of his power at the beginning
of the novel. Five years ago his authority was challenged over the
war with Okperi. He advised Umuaro not to fight for a piece of
land which was not theirs, warning that Ulu would not support an
unjust claim: "Umuaro is today challenging its *chi*. Is there any
man or woman in Umuaro who does not know Ulu, the deity that
destroys a man when his life is sweetest to him? Some people are
still talking of carrying war to Okperi. Do they think that Ulu will
fight in blame? Today the world is spoilt and there is no longer
head or tail in anything that is done. But Ulu is not spoilt with it"
(ii). Nwaka, however, the most titled man in the six villages, refuses to accept the priest's authority. He tells the assembly that
the role of the Chief Priest should be strictly limited to his ritual
and that they do not need to ask his permission before going to
war. "The man who carries a deity is not a king. He is there to
perform its ritual and to carry sacrifice to it. But I have been
watching this Ezeulu for many years. He is a man of ambition; he
wants to be king, priest, diviner, all." Nwaka is even prepared to
attack the deities; as far as he is concerned, their sole function is
to improve the welfare of the tribe. "Let us not listen to anyone
trying to frighten us with the name of Ulu. If a man says yes his
chi also says yes. And we have all heard how the people of Aninta
dealt with their deity when he failed them. Did they not carry
him to the boundary between them and their neighbors and set
fire on him?" (ii). Nwaka won the argument, the war lasted five

days, and was then stopped by the intervention of the white man who broke the guns of the contestants and, after due consideration, awarded the land to Okperi.

Ezeulu looks back with bitter satisfaction on these events. "Umuaro challenged the deity which laid the foundation of their villages. And—what did they expect?—he thrashed them, thrashed them enough for today and tomorrow!" (ii). This has only exacerbated his quarrel with Nwaka and his supporters, which was further intensified by the official inquiry into the ownership of the land at which Ezeulu spoke against his own people. The priest now asks himself in genuine perplexity: "But how could a man who held the holy staff of Ulu know that a thing was a lie and speak it? How could he fail to tell the story as he had heard it from his own father?" (i). Where does his chief responsibility lie, to the tribe or to his god? Since the tribe created Ulu as their protector, is it possible for Ezeulu to support the god against the tribe? The conflict within Umuaro calls into question not only the role of the priest but that of the god himself. The opposing attitudes toward the divine are neatly summed up in the war debate when Ezeulu announces irrevocably, "no matter how strong or great a man was he should never challenge his *chi*," to which, as we have seen, Nwaka replies, "If a man says yes his *chi* also says yes." These two points of view, which jostled one another in *Things Fall Apart,* are now radically opposed. One says that man must be subordinate and subservient to the divine; the other insists that the divine is an expression or an agent of the human. The question of Ezeulu's power is an aspect of this more fundamental problem of the nature of divinity.

The quarrel is not limited to the two men and the god Ulu. It spreads to their respective villages, Umuachala and Umunneora, and it involves Ezidemili who is secretly supporting Nwaka against his rival. He is the priest of Idemili, the personal god of Umunneora, and it is he who prompts Nwaka to query the authority of Ulu and his priest and, as we have seen, to threaten the god with destruction. Ezeulu knows his enemies and the origin of their grievances, but even he is taken aback by their boldness: "He knew that the priests of Idemili and Ogwugwu and Eru and Udo had never been happy with their secondary role since the villages got together and made Ulu and put him over the older deities. But he would not have thought that one of them would go so far

as to get someone to challenge Ulu" (iv). This is the extra ingredient in the quarrel. The handing over of supreme power to Ulu
and his priest was a unique act at a time of crisis, and now the
community is becoming increasingly restless under his inflexible,
non-traditional system of authority.

This is the crisis within the six villages of Umuaro when the
novel opens. It is a struggle for power both on the religious and
the political level, and in the structure of Ibo thought these are
inseparable: powerful gods make powerful priests who make
powerful elders of the tribe. The complexity of this opening situation is controlled by the author's narrative focus. At first we are
confined to the point of view of Ezeulu as he performs his rituals
and broods upon his enemies, and we are encouraged to sympathize with this aged priest who fulfills his religious offices on behalf of the community which challenges his power. Gradually, the
perspective widens and, although Ezeulu remains in the center of
the stage, other characters begin to express their views. As Nwaka
and Ezidemili interpret events from their point of view, we are
encouraged to take up a more detached position and see the
struggle in Umuaro not simply as a crisis in the life of Ezeulu but
as an integral part of the continuing dialectic of power in the
tribe. In addition, Ezeulu the man begins to appear from behind
the priest. As we watch him abusing his senior wife and officiously
reprimanding his sons we begin to see that Umuaro's dilemma is a
matter of personalities as well as of roles.

II   *The District Commissioner*

Umuaro is only one of the worlds of the novel. Achebe presents quite separately the world of the British administrators who
are responsible for ruling this part of Nigeria and whose compla-
cency and ignorance were caught and dismissed with bitter irony
on the last page of *Things Fall Apart*. Now the author attempts
the more difficult task of creating in detail the values, the attitudes, and the atmosphere of this colonial society exercised by the
problems of the dual mandate and indirect rule. In the previous
novel the white man was an eccentric intrusion; here he is shown
to have created in Africa his own rituals and way of life. As
Achebe juxtaposes and then intermingles these two societies, he
creates significant and unexpected perspectives which are the sign
of a new confidence and power.

The chief character in this world is Captain Winterbottom, the District Commissioner, whom we meet on the veranda of his bungalow watching the first rain of the year. Although he is an "Old Coaster" of fifteen years service, Africa is still alien and hostile. As he confronts the Dark Continent we are forcibly reminded of the opening pages of the novel; there, in contrast, Ezeulu was searching the familiar night sky for the new moon, the sign for his ancient ritual. Winterbottom looks out on to a world in which nothing, except its hostility, is taken for granted:

For the past month or two the heat had been building up to an unbearable pitch. The grass had long been burnt out, and the leaves of the more hardy trees had taken on the red and brown earth colour of the country. There was only two hours' respite in the morning before the country turned into a furnace and perspiration came down in little streams from the head and neck. The most exasperating was the little stream that always coursed down behind the ear like a fly, walking. There was another moment of temporary relief at sundown when a cool wind blew. But this treacherous cool wind was the great danger of Africa, beguiling the unwary European who bared himself to it and received its death-kiss. (iii)

After the priest's familiar world, the most striking feature here, is the externality of the landscape and the climate. As the European records the threat of this alien environment, he makes us realize how convincingly normal is the African world which Achebe has created. There, rituals reflect harmoniously the movement of the seasons as the individual and the environment function together; in contrast, the European looks at the landscape as a spectator and sees reflected there his own alienation.

In the middle of the night, physical discomfort turns into something more threatening when Winterbottom hears the inexplicable sounds of the adjacent African world:

At night he had to imprison himself inside a mosquito-net which shut out whatever air movement there was outside. His bedclothes were sodden and his head formed a waterlogged basin on the pillow. After the first stretch of unrestful sleep he would lie awake, tossing about until he was caught in the distant throb of drums. He would wonder what unspeakable rites went on in the forest at night, or was it the heartbeat of the African darkness? . . . Could it be that the throbbing came from his own heat-stricken brain? (iii)

The drum beats, which signified for Ezeulu the ritualistic harmony between man and his environment, threaten Winterbottom's identity as the clear demarcation line between inner and
outer reality becomes blurred. The language is that of Conrad's
Marlow as he sails up the Congo, and, like Kurtz, Winterbottom
has a "strong belief in the value of the British mission in Africa"
(iii). But for the moment he shows no signs of capitulating to the
African darkness; he has more pressing concerns.

Like Ezeulu, he is principally concerned with the problem of
power. A strongminded, authoritarian person, he finds himself being forced to implement the British government's policy of indirect rule which he strongly disapproves of. He is appalled by the
lack of firmness of British policy in Nigeria and the newfangled
ideas which are supplanting the straightforward civilizing mission
of the nineteenth century. As he tells Clarke, his assistant who has
just arrived from England: "We flounder from one expedient to
its opposite. We do not only promise to secure old savage tyrants
on their thrones—or more likely filthy animal skins—we not only
do that, but we now go out of our way to invent chiefs where
there were none before." He objects particularly to these advanced ideas affecting the day-to-day running of the country: "I
wouldn't really mind if this dithering was left to old fossils in
Lagos, but when young Political Officers get infected I just give
up" (iii). Like the Chief Priest of Ulu he rebels against the idea of
becoming simply an intermediary of power, between, in his case,
the British Government and the native chiefs. He looks back nos-
talgically to the days when "the man on the spot," as he calls him,
could act decisively and without restraint. He recalls the time of
Things Fall Apart when his friend George Allen was in Umuofia
and wrote his book, *The Pacification of the Primitive Tribes of the
Lower Niger.* In this way, Achebe employs his first novel to give
an added historical perspective to the problems of colonial policy
in this novel. A passage from Allen's book recaptures the ideals
and motives of the colonial rulers before the days of indirect rule:

For those seeking but a comfortable living and a quiet occupation
Nigeria is closed and will be closed until the earth has lost some of its
deadly fertility and until the people live under something like sanitary
conditions. But for those in search of a strenuous life, for those who can
deal with men as others deal with material, who can grasp great situations, coax events, shape destinies and ride on the crest of the wave of

time Nigeria is holding out her hands. For the men who in India have made the Briton the law-maker, the organizer, the engineer of the world this new, old land has great rewards and honourable work. I know we can find the men. . . . (iii)

Now, a few years later, when pacification has been completed and the soldiers have departed, Clarke finds this rather smug. He says to Winterbottom to whom he is returning the book: "He doesn't allow, for instance, for there being anything of value in native institutions. He might really be one of the missionary people." Infuriated, Winterbottom replies: "I see you are one of the progressive ones. When you've been here as long as Allen was and understood the native a little more you might modify some of your new theories." He clinches his case with a vignette from the life of a man on the spot: "If you saw, as I did, a man buried alive up to his neck with a piece of roast yam on his head to attract vultures you might have second thoughts" (iii). Like Ezeulu, he argues from past experiences which are no longer relevant; authoritarian, middle-aged, and superseded by his junior officers, Winterbottom bitterly resents any change in the hierarchical and familiar power structure which insulates him from the problems of his private life. Indirect rule is far too insecure, too flexible, too reductive of his own status and mission.

Achebe has opposed the two very different worlds of the novel and then skilfully developed this parallelism between his main characters. The problems and complexities of authority and power reveal a surprisingly similar pattern in the colonial and in the tribal world. Both men look back to the heroic days—to the dangerous days of the Abam and to the time of pacification—to justify authoritarian attitudes and systems which are no longer valid. Fixed in their ways, they resist innovations in which they are unwillingly involved: Ezeulu must reluctantly conduct a hostile Umuaro through the rituals of the seasons, while Winterbottom must hand over his authority to bogus native chiefs. Unwillingly they are both becoming involved in the dialectic of power which prevents authority being located in one agent as it was in the days of Ulu's glory and the British pacification. Hence, the vivid particularity of the two disparate worlds of the novel pushes them apart while this common preoccupation of the main characters signifiantly draws them together again. This is a major step in the logic of Achebe's development. Having effortlessly destroyed the myth of African primitivism in *Things Fall Apart,* and established Ibo life as a valid norm, he then traced the effect of two powerful but contradictory cultures upon his hero in *No Longer at Ease.* Now, beneath the hostility of these two cultures, Achebe is beginning to reveal common elements and patterns of meaning. He defines their differences in order to assert more clearly that they are alike.

The world of the Europeans also has its rituals. Although there are only five men on Government Hill in Okperi, Winterbottom insists on the rigid hierarchy of power. There are the administrators, the other officials, and the engineer Wright, the weak link, who Winterbottom feels is letting the side down by his behavior with the native women. He has already had occasion to reprimand him:

It was absolutely imperative, he told him, that every European in Nigeria, particularly those in such a lonely outpost as Okperi, should not lower themselves in the eyes of the natives. In such a place the District Officer was something of a school prefect, and Captain Winterbottom was determined to do his duty. He would go as far as barring Wright from the club unless he showed a marked change. (iii)

This exaggerated formalism, like the rituals of baths and dressing for dinner, is a means of keeping isolation and alienation at bay. It is only in the small hours that Winterbottom wonders if the distant throb of drums originates in his own fevered brain.

Parody of this kind is integral to a novel created out of the juxtaposition of two incompatible societies. It expresses the discrepancy between the inside and the outside view. As the Europeans employ their defensive strategies against the unknown, their simplifications and exaggerations are pushed into parody by our inside view of the African society which has elicited them. The rich texture of Ibo traditional life is reduced before our eyes to the simple outline of the stereotype. From Government Hill, Ezeulu's familiar rituals become the unspeakable rites of the heart of darkness. This does not mean that Achebe depicts the Europeans as a beleaguered minority of extreme reactionaries. Winterbottom, Clarke, and Wright represent different colonial points of view. Winterbottom himself is not simply an embittered "Old Coaster"; he knows the country well, understands the Ibo language, and acts according to the values he believes in. And parody works in the opposite direction too. The villagers assume similarly defensive and exaggerated postures later in the novel when they seek to contain the encroachments of the Europeans. So long as the two worlds of the novel remain unintelligible to each other they act in a similar way in face of the unknown. The Europeans seek refuge behind their myths and rituals as they strive to administer this corner of empire. They are looking for a power structure they can understand and promote: if they cannot find one, they will have to create it. The Ibo use ritual as a safeguard against the Europeans, but mainly to placate the mysterious spirit world which surrounds them. This is the reality they spend the greater part of their lives grappling with. The result of this separation is mutual misunderstanding, and so, despite their similar problems and ambitions, the two worlds never achieve any insight into each other's systems of value.

Mutual misinterpretation is, in fact, the chief structural device of the novel. The same sequence of events is deciphered according to very different systems of value and the repercussions on future events traced. We have seen, for example, how Ezeulu regarded the intervention of "Wintabota" in the war with Okperi; as far as he was concerned, the punishment of Umuaro validated the authority of Ulu which had been challenged. Now Winterbottom gives us the European version as he shows Clarke his collection of queer-looking guns:

Those guns have a long and interesting history. The people of Okperi and their neighbours, Umuaro, are great enemies. Or they were before I came into the story. A big savage war had broken out between them over a piece of land. This feud was made worse by the fact that Okperi welcomed missionaries and government while Umuaro, on the other hand, has remained backward. It was only in the last four or five years that any kind of impression has been made there. I think I can say with all modesty that this change came after I had gathered and publicly destroyed all firearms in the place except, of course, this collection here. (iii)

Winterbottom sees these events as an interesting episode in his life history and an opportunity to display his knowledge of the natives. Achebe captures well the bluff, pompous, and condescending style of the district commissioner as he translates the complex network of events into colonial logic. For the Ibo the violence is the work of Ekwensu, the bringer of evil; Winterbottom attributes it to palm-wine.

As I was saying, this war started because a man from Umuaro went to visit a friend in Okperi one fine morning and after he'd had one or two gallons of palm-wine—it's quite incredible how much of that dreadful stuff they can tuck away—anyhow, this man from Umuaro having drunk his friend's palm-wine reached for his *ikenga* and split it in two. I may explain that *ikenga* is the most important fetish in the Ibo man's arsenal, so to speak. It represents his ancestors to whom he must make daily sacrifice. When he dies it is split in two; one half is buried with him and the other half is thrown away. So you can see the implication of what our friend from Umuaro did in splitting his host's fetish. This was, of course, the greatest sacrilege. The outraged host reached for his gun and blew the other fellow's head off. And so a regular war developed between the two villages, until I stepped in.

The two versions do overlap to some extent. Winterbottom understands the importance of the *ikenga,* but his explanation is essentially secular. This is why his account of the chain of cause and effect peters out in the fortuitous drunken act of the man from Umuaro. This is supported by the administrator's mistrust of the troublemakers of Umuaro who refuse to cooperate with the Europeans. In Ezeulu's version, of course, the flaunting of Ulu's authority both causes and determines the result of the war; the white man becomes unwittingly the agent of the god. Yet despite their different interpretations, the two men are prompted by very similar motives. Ezeulu refuses to abrogate one iota of the authority invested in Ulu and by extension in himself: Winterbottom uses the episode as convincing evidence of the need for direct rule by the administrator on the spot. Perhaps this is why Winterbottom experiences a moment of sympathy for his African counterpart at the subsequent official inquiry. He ends his account in this way:

I should mention that every witness who testified before me—from both sides without exception—perjured themselves. One thing you must remember in dealing with natives is that like children they are great liars. They don't lie simply to get out of trouble. Sometimes they would spoil a good case by a pointless lie. Only one man—a kind of priest-king in Umuaro—witnessed against his own people. I have not found out what it was, but I think he must have had some pretty fierce tabu working on him. But he was a most impressive figure of a man. He was very light in complexion, almost red. (iii)

He doesn't realize that this was part of Ezeulu's personal campaign to re-establish the unique prestige of Ulu. Yet he grudgingly admires a man of authority witnessing to the truth against his own people's misguided views; no doubt, he sees himself playing a similar misunderstood role. And his admiration is reciprocated. Ezeulu derives great satisfaction from the support he, in turn, received from the white man: "But how could a man who held the holy staff of Ulu know that a thing was a lie and speak it? . . . Even the white man, Wintabota, understood, though he came from a land no one knew. He had called Ezeulu the only witness of truth" (i). They misunderstand each other's motives but achieve a kind of rapport; they also influence each other's exercise of power. Winterbottom's judgment against Umuaro exonerates Ulu and his priest, while Ezeulu's testimony at the inquiry enables Winterbottom to expedite the implementation of indirect rule.

Winterbottom has just received an abrupt reminder, in the shape of a memorandum from the lieutenant-governor, to speed up the appointment of two warrant chiefs in his district. To the accompaniment of the singing of prisoners who are cutting his grass ("When I cut grass and you cut? What's your right to call me names?"), he impatiently reads the latest "progressive" statement from Government House.

My purpose in these paragraphs is limited to impressing on all Political Officers working among tribes who lack Natural Rulers the vital necessity of developing without any further delay an effective system of "indirect rule" based on native institutions. . . . In place of the alternative of governing directly through Administrative Officers there is the other method of trying while we endeavour to purge the native system of its abuses to build a higher civilization upon the soundly rooted native stock that had its foundation in the hearts and minds and thoughts of the people and therefore on which we can more easily build, moulding it and establishing it into lines consonant with modern ideas and higher standards, and yet all the time enlisting the real force of the spirit of the people, instead of killing all that out and trying to start afresh. We must not destroy the African atmosphere, the African mind, the whole foundation of his race. . . . (v)

The inflated language of George Allen's stirring call to action has
been modified; the existing society is to be allowed to assist the
civilizing mission. The problem, as Winterbottom sees it, is the
absence among the Ibo of these so-called natural rulers one finds
in other parts of Africa. These are the men traditionally respected
by the class-conscious, conservative administrators of the colonial
service. Tribes without such rulers and the hierarchical system
which creates them have been customarily dismissed as backward
and anarchic. Winterbottom hands on this conventional view to
Clarke: "Unlike some of the more advanced tribes in Northern
Nigeria, and to some extent Western Nigeria, the Ibos never developed any kind of central authority." He has failed to discrimi-
nate between anarchy and the subtle dialectic continually at work
between the different power groups of Ibo society which pre-
serves, as we saw in *Things Fall Apart,* its flexibility and openness.
In consequence, Winterbottom's quest for a Paramount Chief in
Umuaro is doubly difficult: he has to find an authoritative leader
in a segmented society which he misunderstands. And he has one
mistake already to his credit in the appointment of the Chief for
Okperi who, he remembers, quickly set up an illegal court and
private prison, and organized a system of mass extortion. "This
was what British administration was doing among the Ibos, making a dozen mushroom kings grow where there was none before"
(v). Now Winterbottom has, reluctantly, another chance. As he
muses over the appointment to be made in Okperi he recalls
Ezeulu's testimony five years ago and his mind focuses rather
hazily on the neighboring world of Umuaro:

He was now under orders to find a chief and his duty was clear. But
he must not repeat the mistake of looking for a mission-educated smart
alec. As far as Umuaro was concerned his mind was practically made
up. He would go for that impressive-looking fetish priest who alone of
all the witnesses who came before him in the Okperi versus Umuaro
land case spoke the truth. Provided of course he was still alive. Captain
Winterbottom remembered seeing him again once or twice during his
routine visits to Umuaro. But that was at least two years ago. (v)

Winterbottom clearly feels that it might not be too painful to
hand over power to the "impressive-looking fetish priest" who
seems to understand the white man's justice. In this way, as the
two main characters jealously safeguard the authority which has

been entrusted to them, they both find reassurance in the land
inquiry which fits conveniently into their very different patterns of
meaning. And for the moment it does seem as if the aims of the
two men coincide: Winterbottom wishes to invest Ezeulu with the
authority he so much desires. But the inquiry, the only occasion
on which the two men meet in the novel, contains something more
—a moment of rapport between two strongminded men of power
whose authority is being questioned. As the similarities become
clear it is with an effort that we remind ourselves that one
character inhibits a world of gods, priests, and *ikenga,* the other a
world of government memoranda, district commissioners, and de-
layed promotion.

III   *The Missionaries*

Although they are both involved in the problems of power, the
African and European worlds of the novel misunderstand each
other's motives because, in the last resort, they employ different
frames of reference. The values of Umuaro are finally religious,
those of the colonial administration secular. This is the reason why
they do not see each other as rivals. No such neutrality is observed
by the third group of characters, the missionaries. Mainly Ibos,
but accepting the god brought by the Europeans, they form an
intermediate society between the Africans and the administrators.
They are in direct competition with the priests and tribal deities
for the loyalty of the people. At first, they seem peripheral to the
main events of the novel, impinging only slightly on the major
characters. Ezeulu might hear the sounds of their ritual as he
meditates on his priestly role, but he is not unduly perturbed:
"The place where the Christians built their place of worship was
not far from Ezeulu's compound. As he sat in his *obi* thinking of
the Festival of the Pumpkin Leaves he heard their bell: GOME,
GOME, GOME, GOME, GOME. His mind turned from the festival to
the new religion. He was not sure what to make of it" (iv). The
only precaution he has taken is to send with some misgivings his
third son, Oduche, to join the missionaries. He tells him: "If there
is nothing in it you will come back. But if there is something there
you will bring home my share. The world is like a Mask dancing.
If you want to see it well you do not stand in one place. My spirit
tells me that those who do not befriend the white man today will
be saying *had we known* tomorrow" (iv). He is seeking to insure

himself against any possible rivals in Umuaro, and his fears prove well founded. The Christian bell rings in an increasingly peremptory fashion as the divisions between the six villages deepen.

But the missionaries have their own internal disagreements. Like Umuaro and the British administration, they are engaged in a dispute over the best way of exercising and extending their power. The catechist John Goodcountry from the Niger Delta means to rout pagan superstition by his uncompromising, literal Christianity. He despises the traditional beliefs of Umuaro and looks back with admiration to the early Christians "who fought the bad customs of their people, destroyed shrines and killed the sacred iguana." This aggressive missionary justifies himself by means of biblical myth: "You must be ready to kill the python as the people of the rivers killed the iguana. You address the python as Father. It is nothing but a snake, the snake that deceived our first mother, Eve" (iv). But Moses Unachukwu, the pastor's warden, disagrees with this violent campaign of conversion. He too values the myths of the Bible—he has spent ten years as a carpenter with the white man—but he does not see why these are incompatible with the myths of Umuaro. He challenges Goodcountry's attack upon the sacred python of Idemili: "To do this he used not only the Bible but, strangely enough for a convert, the myths of Umuaro. He spoke with great power for, coming as he did from the village which carried the priesthood of Idemili, he knew perhaps more than others what the python was. On the other side, his great knowledge of the Bible and his sojourn in Onitsha which was the source of the new religion gave him great confidence. He told the new teacher quite bluntly that neither the Bible nor the catechism asked converts to kill the python, a beast full of ill omen" (iv).

At this point in the debate, Oduche intervenes and justifies Ezeulu's earlier misgivings. He has become a committed Christian and now contradicts Unachukwu's argument by a use of biblical text as literal as Goodcountry's: "It is not true that the Bible does not ask us to kill the serpent. Did not God tell Adam to crush the serpent which deceived his wife?" The bitter exchange which follows ends when Unachukwu turns on Oduche and challenges him to kill a python in Umuaro. Oduche is determined to accept the challenge, but gradually the sanctions of Umuaro undermine his resolution. Finally, he compromises by locking a sacred python in the wooden box made for each convert by the mission carpenter: "The python would die for lack of air, and he would be responsible for its death without being guilty of killing it. In the ambivalence of his present life his act seemed to him a very happy compromise" (iv). His father in a rage frees the exhausted python and Oduche is held by the clan to have insulted Ezidemili and his god. In this way, the excursion into the Christian world of the novel is brought back to the more central tribal world where the main struggle for power is taking place. Not more central, of course, to the Christians. As far as they are concerned, the struggles between competing tribal deities is further evidence that Umuaro needs the Christian God.

The introduction of this third missionary world opens up new perspectives in the novel. Instead of seeing Umuaro as a political unit as the colonial administrators do, we are now encouraged to understand its problems as those of a religious sect. It is, of course, both, and in this way Achebe can stress first one and then the other of its major concerns. In addition, the missionary world extends the definition of the general themes we noticed earlier. We have examined the similarities between Ezeulu's world and Winterbottom's where direct control was opposed by a more reciprocal distribution of power—either by the dialectic of the tribe or indirect rule. When we move into the world of the Christian missionaries the central concern is the power of conversion. Despite this displacement, the theme is the same: By what means are power and influence best exerted? Again, there are two alternatives. There is the direct imposition of alien values which ignores the beliefs of the community; or there is persuasion through negotiation with existing values. The first is based on a belief in the absoluteness of power, truth, and civilization; the second on a belief in the relativity of these abstractions which are only realized through particular relationships. One is unilateral in its mode, the other dialectical. This opposition was first examined in Okonkwo's career in *Things Fall Apart* where it arose from the clash between the hero's character and Ibo society. Such a clash also occurs in this novel between Ezeulu and the mores of Umuaro. But now Achebe is prepared to generalize more freely outside the confines of tribal life: colonial rule and Christian proselytizing are shown to display the same tension between alternative modes of action.

The interaction of the three worlds of the novel is controlled by

these internal, analogous conflicts. We have seen this already in
the dealings between Winterbottom and Ezeulu. The same is true
in this clash between Umuaro and the missionaries: Oduche's
presence among the missionaries is prompted by his father's need
for power, while his insult to the python springs from the dissen-
sions in the mission. The clash which ensues precipitates further
events which sharpen the distinctions between different modes of
action. In this case, after Oduche's sacrilegious act, Ezeulu is
questioned by his friend Akuebe about the present problems of
Umuaro. Akuebe is disturbed by Oduche's action; he understood
that Ezeulu's son had been sent to learn the secrets of the white
man's magic, not to insult the religion of his own people and
worsen relations between his father and Ezidemili. Ezeulu immediately interprets these complaints as another attempt by his enemies in Umuaro to curb his power: "I am not blind and I am not
deaf either. I know that Umuaro is divided and confused and I
know that some people are holding secret meetings to persuade
others that I am the cause of the trouble." In his disdain he speaks
as if he is above such criticism, as if his rectitude in the last war
exonerates him from any further involvement. "Did I not stand up
then and tell Umuaro what would happen to them? And who was
right in the end? What I said, did it happen or did it not?" (xii).
The self-righteousness of this reply is too much for his friend.
Akuebe repeats to Ezeulu the warning that is reiterated throughout the novel: "I do not doubt that . . . but you forget one thing:
that no man however great can win judgment against a clan. You
may think you did in that land dispute but you are wrong.
Umuaro will always say that you betrayed them before the white
man. And they will say that you are betraying them again today
by sending your son to join in desecrating the land." We are back
to the opening questions of the novel about the nature of the
priest's power. Akuebe is trying to convince his friend that his
power is not absolute but dependent upon the consent of the
tribe.

   In his reply, Ezeulu condescendingly explains in his most oracular manner that he is pursuing a policy which mere mortals cannot
comprehend: "I have my own way and I shall follow it. I can see
things where other men are blind. That is why I am Known and at
the same time I am Unknowable . . . you cannot know the
Thing which beats the drum to which Ezeulu dances." As chief

priest he is seeking the welfare of the whole tribe; he is not using his son against Ezidemili but as a sacrifice for the safety of Umuaro, just as their ancestors "when they were pushed beyond the end of things by the warriors of Abam sacrificed not a stranger but one of themselves and made the great medicine which they called Ulu" (xii). But he does not consider himself answerable to the tribe since he is moving in a world, half spirit and half human, which is not explicable in terms of local rivalries.

Ezeulu's answer reminds Akuebe of the second matter he wishes to raise. Edogo, the priest's eldest son, has complained that his father is seeking to determine the will of Ulu in the choice of his successor. Akuebe asks, "What happens if this boy you are sacrificing turns out to be the chosen by Ulu when you are looked for and not found?" The answer comes pat: "Leave that to the deity. When the time comes of which you speak Ulu will not seek your advice or help" (xii). Akeube is impressed by the priest's authority, but he warns him against alienating the tribe from whom he derives his power. Without its support he would be alone and helpless. Ezeulu's rejoinder is again contemptuous: "As for being alone, do you not think that it should be as familiar to me now as are dead bodies to the earth? My friend, don't make me laugh." This disagreement over the priest's successor enables us to examine the problem of Ezeulu's role from within the family. Edogo is in no doubt that he and his brothers are being manipulated, not by Ulu, but by their father's ambitions. He remembers his mother used to say "that Ezeulu's only fault was that he expected everyone . . . to think and act like himself. Anyone who dared to say no to him was an enemy. He forgot the saying of the elders that if a man sought for a companion who acted entirely like himself he would live in solitude" (ix). This view translates the priest's conduct into easily recognized human terms and it must be added to the views of his friends, his rivals, the white man and the missionaries.

Ezeulu is clearly trying to answer by his actions the question posed at the beginning of the novel: "What kind of power was it if everybody knew that it would never be used?" As he becomes more and more isolated in his self-righteousness, he is less tolerant of any restraint by his family or the tribe. He is convinced that he is the agent of Ulu acting according to a logic the villagers cannot understand. When they question his motives, his strategy is to

shift rapidly from his human to his priestly role, from the secular
to the divine frame of reference. This is how he justifies his conduct at the land case, his despatch of Oduche to the Christians,
his manipulation of his other three sons. We are not allowed to see
inside Ezeulu's mind as he makes this mental shift and consequently cannot say how self-conscious is this technique of self-
justification. For the most part he seems to translate his own
wishes and those of his god into each other effortlessly, but his
motives remain ambiguous. As he seeks to extend his influence
into the adjacent worlds of the white man and the missionaries,
Ezeulu becomes more isolated and disregardful of the tribe which
is querying his motives with increasing skepticism.

IV   *The Death of Ulu*

At this critical stage in the relationship of the priest and the
tribe, the European world intervenes. Winterbottom decides reluctantly that he must expedite the new policy of Indirect Rule he
so mistrusts. He sends for Ezeulu to Okperi in order to make him
warrant chief in Umuaro. Unfortunately, the court messenger
who brings the summons arrogantly adopts the manners and
methods of his white master. Ezeulu takes umbrage and proudly
rejects Winterbottom's order: "tell your white man that Ezeulu
does not leave his hut. If he wants to see me he must come here"
(xii). Ironically, Ezeulu deprives himself in this way of power
within a system of government free from the exasperating checks
and balances endemic to the Ibo. But at this point he is more
intent on forcing an issue with his rivals in Umuaro. Are they
prepared to support their Chief Priest in this new opposition to
the white man? He calls the clan together and asks this question.
The reply comes from his chief rival, Nwaka, who reminds everyone sarcastically of Ezeulu's previous affiliations: "The white man
is Ezeulu's friend and has sent for him. What is so strange about
that? . . . I have heard one or two voices murmuring that it is
against custom for the priest of Ulu to travel far from his hut. I
want to ask such people: Is this the first time Ezeulu would be
going to Okperi? Who was the white man's witness that year we
fought for our land—and lost?" (xiii). Again Achebe has presented two interpretations of the priest's motives. According to
the logic of his priesthood, he is acting quite consistently: he must
speak the truth as Ulu decrees and he must not obey any authority

but that of his god. But his actions can be construed more simply as self-interest. When the clan inclines to the second view, Ezeulu knows with some satisfaction that the time has come to force the dispute with his people to a final issue. On the next morning he walks to Okperi and hands himself over to the district commissioner who has just signed a warrant for his arrest.

Winterbottom has come to accept Indirect Rule as a necessary evil when this "self-important fetish priest" dares to insult him in this way. He is apoplectic with rage and orders him to be locked in the guardroom. In their arrogant display of power both men are quite ignorant of the adjacent power structure which is continually interfering with their plans in a mysterious way. The irony of the situation is underlined by the similarity in the attitudes of the two men and, on this occasion, by the results of their interference. By jailing Ezeulu, Winterbottom prevents him from carrying out the rituals in Umuaro he is chafing under; by refusing to cooperate with the administration, Ezeulu prevents Winterbottom putting into practice the system of Indirect Rule he finds so objectionable. An appreciation of this symmetry is, of course, denied to the participants. The only effect on Winterbottom is rage and frenzy which brings on his next bout of fever and convinces his servants that Ezeulu has struck him down: "the priest had hit him with a potent charm. In spite of everything then, power still resided in its accustomed place." They pay a visit to the local *dibia* who gives them, on payment of two cocks, a magic preparation to drink and mix in their bath water. Then, unlike the presumptuous main characters, they have secured their safety within both systems of power. Their alarm is finely managed by Achebe as they are shunted between the two authorities.

There was a Court Messenger outside his bungalow when he got home.

" 'Deven sah," said the man.

"Good evening," replied Clarke.

"De witch-doctor from Umuaro don come." There was fear in his voice as though he was reporting the arrival of smallpox in the village.

"I beg your pardon."

The man gave more details and it was only then that Clarke understood he was talking about Ezeulu.

"Lock him in the guardroom till morning." Clarke made to enter the bungalow.

"Massa say make I putam for gaddaloom?"
"That's what I said," shouted Clarke. "Are you deaf?"
"No be say I deaf sah but . . ."
"Get out!" (xiii)

Imprisoned at Okperi, Ezeulu's isolation within his own bitterness is complete. He is now more than ever convinced that Ulu is using him to punish the clan which has flaunted his authority. A nightmare in which Umuaro openly insults the god finally corroborates all his suspicions. Nwaka asks, "Is there anybody here who cannot see the moon in his own compound? And anyhow what is the power of Ulu today?" and then the people spat in the face of the Chief Priest and "called him the priest of a dead god" (xiv). This horrifying vision directs Ezeulu to thoughts of revenge; he realizes that his quarrel with the white man is insignificant compared with the enormity of the crime of Umuaro. "For years he had been warning Umuaro not to allow a few jealous men to lead them into the bush. But they had stopped both ears with fingers. They had gone on taking one dangerous step after another and now they had gone too far. . . . Ezeulu's muscles tingled for the fight. Let the white man detain him not for one day but one year so that his deity not seeing him in his place would ask Umuaro questions" (xiv).

When at last he is offered the post of warrant chief, he is so obsessed with his revenge against Umuaro that he evinces little interest.

The expression on the priest's face did not change when the news was broken to him. He remained silent. Clarke knew it would take a little time for the proposal to strike him with its full weight.

"Well, are you accepting the offer or not?" Clarke glowed with the I-know-this-will-knock-you-over feeling of a benefactor.

"Tell the white man that Ezeulu will not be anybody's chief, except Ulu."

"What!" shouted Clarke. "Is the fellow mad?"

"I tink so sah," said the interpreter.

"In that case he goes back to prison." Clarke was now really angry. What cheek! A witch-doctor making a fool of the British Administration in public! (xiv)

Unwilling as he is to share any of his priestly direct rule, Ezeulu certainly does not want to participate in an alien system of indirect rule. But he is too preoccupied to be even antagonized by this treatment. Everything is working together for the exoneration of Ulu: "his real struggle was with his own people and the white man was, without knowing it, his ally. The longer he was kept in Okperi the greater his grievance and his resources for the fight" (xv). He is utterly convinced that he is indispensable to the life of Umuaro. After thirty-two days he is set free by Clarke who has now taken over from the sick Winterbottom; his release has been hastened by an adverse report from the Secretary for Native Affairs on Indirect Rule in Eastern Nigeria. At the present time "it was clearly inadvisable to extend the appointment of Warrant Chiefs to new areas" (xv). Ezeulu returns home to confront the recalcitrant clan and the final, most impressive phase of the novel begins.

The overwhelming welcome he receives on his return undermines his resolve. He is brought to realize that in his isolation he simplified the hostility of Umuaro, that there are in fact many villagers who still support him. "From the moment he made this division thoughts of reconciliation began, albeit timidly, to visit him" (xvi). Perhaps Umuaro misunderstood the logic of his priestly actions. As he re-establishes contact with his friends, he comes to accept with a certain amount of pride their view that no one else could have wrestled with and defeated the white man as he had done.

Yes, it was right that the Chief Priest should go ahead and confront danger before it reached his people. That was the responsibility of his priesthood. It had been like that from the first day when the six harassed villages got together and said to Ezeulu's ancestor: "You will carry this deity for us." At first he was afraid. What power had he in his body to carry such potent danger? But his people sang their support behind him and the flute man turned his head. So he went down on both knees and they put the deity on his head. He rose up and was transformed into a spirit. His people kept up their song behind him and he stepped forward on his first and decisive journey, compelling even the four days in the sky to give way to him. (xvi)

For the only time in the novel Ezeulu divests himself of his traditional authority, goes back in time to the creation of Ulu, and relives the unique ceremony from the point of view of the frightened villager, his ancestor, who was transformed into a spirit. At this impressive moment he sees himself not as a servant of the god but as the representative of the people who have created both god and priest. The nightmare vision of Ulu's dethronement is superseded by this imaginative re-creation of tribal harmony. The traditional Ibo warning—"no man however great can win judgement against a clan"—has been converted into a source of strength. Now that he has achieved a reciprocity between his human and divine roles, Ezeulu no longer feels the need to show that his power over the tribe is absolute.

He is not allowed to enjoy his newfound sense of community for long. As he is sitting in his compound, beginning "to probe with the sensitiveness of a snail's horns the possibility of reconciliation, or, if that was too much, of narrowing down the area of conflict," Ulu himself makes his one direct intervention in the novel and speaks to his priest.

"Ta! Nwanu!" barked Ulu in his ear, as a spirit would in the ear of an impertinent human child. "Who told you that this was your own fight?"

Ezeulu trembled and said nothing.

"I say who told you that this was your own fight which you could arrange to suit you? You want to save your friends who brought you palm wine he-he-he-he-he!" laughed the deity the way spirits do—a dry, skeletal laugh. "Beware you do not come between me and my victim or you may receive blows not meant for you! Do you not know what happens when two elephants fight? Go home and sleep and leave me to settle my quarrel with Idemili, who wants to destroy me so that his python may come to power. Now you tell me how it concerns you. I say go home and sleep." (xvi)

Ulu has reasserted his control over the divine half of Ezeulu's ambiguous nature in an unmistakable way, and all doubts and perplexities are resolved. The priest again becomes the remote agent of Ulu: "After that there was no more to be said. Who was Ezeulu to tell his deity how to fight the jealous cult of the sacred python? It was a fight of the gods. He was no more than an arrow in the bow of his god. The thought intoxicated Ezeulu like palm wine" (xvi).

Now the ambiguity of recent events can be cleared up. "New thoughts tumbled over themselves and past events took on a new, exciting significance." Oduche was clearly being used against

Idemili, and the white man too can now be seen as an instrument
of Ulu's will: "After all he had once taken sides with Ezeulu and,
in a way, had taken sides with him again lately by exiling him,
thus giving him a weapon with which to fight his enemies" (xvi).
The radical new perspective created by Ulu's intervention offers a
far more satisfactory pattern of meaning in which everything is
subordinate to the conflict with the rival god. Ezeulu must now
seize this weapon which has been offered by his imprisonment
and exact punishment on Umuaro which has dared to divide its
loyalty with the sacred python of Idemili. He decides to attack the
clan at its most vulnerable point—the Feast of the New Yam. He
refuses to announce the feast which controls the harvest: "I only
call a new festival when there is only one yam left. Today I have
three yams, and so I know that the time has not come." On behalf
of Ulu he means to make them wait the two extra moons he needs
to eat the remaining sacred yams: "Ulu did say that two new
moons came and went and there was no one to break kolanut to
him and Umuaro kept silent" (xviii). Now the battle is joined and
as the yam harvest begins to rot in the ground and Ezeulu remains
implacable, the question of his power over the clan has to be decided one way or the other. Is it absolute or conditional upon the
consent of Umuaro? The questions on the opening pages of the
novel have a new relevance. "If he should refuse to name the day
there would be no festival—no planting and no reaping. But
could he refuse? No Chief Priest had ever refused. So it could not
be done." He has been forced to refuse and now seeks to prove
that the ritual which governs the life of the clan is in the sole
hands of the god.

With growing desperation the elders suggest various ways of
resolving the deadlock. To all of these Ezeulu replies unrelent-
ingly: "I am the Chief Priest of Ulu and what I have told you is
his will not mine." He remains unmoved and unintimidated when
they remind him that customs have often been changed in the
past, "when they began to work hardship on the people" (xviii).
The traditional reciprocity of tribe and god is of no interest to
him, for at last he is exercising power in an unequivocal way. And
yet as he becomes more and more isolated in his rectitude and the
suffering in Umuaro increases he does feel a deep compassion for
the clan. Only he has understood the extent of Ulu's wrath: "What
troubled him most . . . was that the punishment was not for

now alone but for all time. It would afflict Umuaro like an *ogulu-aro* disease which counts a year and returns to its victim" (xix). In other words, the season and the yam harvest will be permanently out of joint.

Ezeulu's friends believe he is helpless but his enemies interpret his actions as personal revenge. Murmurs of rebellion increase as the dialectic between the tribe and the god begins to function despite the priest's unilateral action. "A priest like Ezeulu leads a god to ruin himself." "Or perhaps a god like Ulu leads a priest to ruin himself" (xviii). Amid this discord, the missionaries, no longer seen as the chief enemy of Umuaro, begin to seize their opportunity. With the same skill he displayed in *Things Fall Apart* Achebe insinuates their growing challenge into the crisis. We begin to hear the sound of the mission bell in the very heart of Umuaro, within the sacred shrine of Ulu. A powerful effect is again achieved when adjacent worlds of the novel come briefly into contact and challenge each other's status quo:

From the rafters right round the room the skulls of all past chief priests looked down on the mound and on their descendant and successor. Even in the hottest day a damp chill always possessed the shrine because of the giant trees outside which put their heads together to cut off the sun, but more especially because of the great, cold, underground river flowing under the earth mound. Even the approaches to the shrine were cold and, all year round, there was always some *ntu-nanya-mili* dropping tears from the top of the ancient trees.

As Ezeulu cast his string of cowries the bell of Oduche's people began to ring. For one brief moment Ezeulu was distracted by its sad, measured monotone and he thought how strange it was that it should sound so near—much nearer than it did in his compound. (xviii)

Thanks to Moses Unachukwu who has been moderating its extreme evangelical zeal, the mission church has been growing in strength. Now, at this point of deadlock, the missionaries intervene and proffer their own harvest festival in lieu of the New Yam festival denied to Umuaro: "whoever made his thank-offering to God could harvest his crops without fear of Ulu" (xviii). The news of the offer spreads as the suffering among the villagers increases.

The climax occurs at the next new moon. Ezeulu eats the twelfth yam and announces the New Yam feast in a month's time.

Then he experiences one of his nightmare visions which he himself links with the fits of madness his mother used to experience at
the new moon, when old songs "forced themselves out in eccentric
spurts through the cracks in her mind." His dream is in two parts.
First he hears a burial party singing the song of Idemili as they
trespass in his compound:

> Look! a python
> Look! a python
> Yes, it lies across the way.

He seeks help but finds in a panic that his *obi* is abandoned and
overgrown. Into this desolation breaks the voice of a solitary
singer in distress; it is the sacred python of Idemili announcing
the common enemy of all the gods of Umuaro.

> I was born when lizards were in ones and twos
> A child of Idemili. The difficult tear-drops
> Of Sky's first weeping drew my spots. Being
> Sky-born I walked the earth with royal gait
> And mourners saw me coiled across their path.
> But of late
> A strange bell
> Has been ringing a song of desolation:
> > Leave your yams and cocoyams
> > And come to school.
> And I must scuttle away in haste
> When children in play or in earnest cry:
> > Look! a Christian is on the way.
> Ha ha ha ha ha ha ha ha ha ha ha ha ha ha . . . (xix)

The Christian god, even in a children's joke, is far more inimical
to Umuaro than its own local rivalries. But Ezeulu does not heed
the warning because it comes, like his mother's songs, in one of
these clearsighted moments of insanity when his waking self is in
abeyance.

The sudden death of Obika picks up this hint of madness in
Ezeulu's family and finally resolves the tensions which have built
up between Ulu, his priest, and the clan. Suffering from a fever,
Obika agrees to perform the role of night spirit in a second burial
ceremony. As he runs round the village he becomes possessed by

the spirit ("He felt like two separate persons, one running above the other") and then collapses and dies. At this supreme moment of crisis within Umuaro the event can only be interpreted in one way—Ulu disapproves of the conduct of his Chief Priest. Fully committed in his self-righteousness to the role of arrow of Ulu, Ezeulu is desolated.

At any other time Ezeulu would have been more than equal to his grief. He would have been equal to any grief not compounded with humiliation. Why, he asked himself again and again, why had Ulu chosen to deal thus with him, to strike him down and cover him with mud? What was his offence? Had he not divined the god's will and obeyed it? When was it ever heard that a child was scalded by the piece of yam its own mother put in its palm? . . . But today such a thing had happened before the eyes of all. What could it point to but the collapse and ruin of all things? (xix)

He is convinced he has obeyed the will of Ulu and yet the god who controls all things in Umuaro has punished him. For Ezeulu this represents a breakdown in the scheme of things; and since he has severed his links with the clan there is no redress. He goes mad and lives out his last days "in the haughty splendour of a demented high priest." Achebe offers us two explanations for his madness as he does for so many other events in the novel, the supernatural and the psychological. "Perhaps it was the constant, futile throbbing of these thoughts that finally left a crack in Ezeulu's mind. Or perhaps his implacable assailant having stood over him for a little while stepped on him as on an insect and crushed him in the dust?" (xix). In the last resort these explanations are not very different. From the first, Ezeulu has wished to impose his authority by direct rule upon the clan. Rejecting the dialectical sharing of power, he has continually and persistently tried to abstract the office of Chief Priest from the tangled obligations of Umuaro. To achieve this he has identified himself completely with Ulu and become the arrow in his bow. But such a simplification of the complex relationship between tribe and god was doomed to failure, and the failure can be expressed in two ways. One can say that either Ezeulu's self-contained egocentric world was bound, sooner or later, to be disrupted by the intractableness of events, or that the powerful god turned against his priest.

Ezeulu's madness spares him the knowledge of the final defeat of his god. The tribe is now convinced that Ulu has punished his priest in accordance with their traditional belief "that no man however great was greater than his people; that no man ever won judgement against his clan" (xix). But Ulu has chosen a dangerous time to destroy his agent in Umuaro. At this critical moment the villagers desperately need permission to harvest their yams, and the missionaries, who are no longer aggressively imposing their religion upon Umuaro, are ready to help. They offer their own harvest festival as an alternative to the festival of the New Yam, and, with relief, the villagers free themselves from a ritual which has become an imprisonment. "In his extremity many an Umuaro man had sent his son with a yam or two to offer to the new religion and to bring back the promised immunity. Thereafter any yam that was harvested in the man's fields was harvested in the name of the son" (xix).

It is now possible to describe in more general terms Achebe's achievement in this novel. He has described the world of colonial administration in Africa in the 1920's at a time of crucial change— the transition from Direct to Indirect Rule. Alongside he has placed the Ibo world of Umuaro at a period of similar crisis—the birth and death of its supreme god. In each world, the direct imposition of authority is challenged by a more realistic and sophisticated view based on the reciprocity of power. The authoritarian agent, in seeking to escape from the uncertainties of the new situation, identifies himself with the source of his power and resists involvement in an uncertain dialectic. Each man becomes vulnerable through the rigidity of his view; in demanding that the world conform to their premises they become the victims of contingency. Ezeulu creates a fully determined world controlled by Ulu and then is destroyed by the inexplicableness of events. The intransigence of events renders Winterbottom helpless in a similar way: "It looked as though the gods and the powers of event finding Winterbottom handy had used him and left him in order as they found him" (xix). The inexplicable events they seek to control arise from the adjacent yet opaque worlds of the novel. This is the irony of the structure of *Arrow of God:* the reader's double perspective transforms the alien and the contingent into the familiar and the explicable. The irony is directed against the characters who insist upon imposing a unitary meaning upon a complex, changing reality. The officials of the intermediate world of the Christian mission extend their power by learning to negotiate in a flexible way with alien myths and to supply their inadequacies.

This, then, is a political novel in which different systems of power are examined and their dependence upon myth and ritual compared. Of necessity, it is also a study in the psychology of power. The authoritarianism of the major characters springs not only from the power structures within which they are operating but also from their personalities. Achebe, however, does not explore the inner worlds which they are seeking to express in politics and religion. We are given terse indications of inner conflict—Ulu reprimands his priest, and the hostile climate finally defeats Winterbottom—but we are only permitted to witness the final disharmony between inner and external reality from the outside. An excessive strain is placed consequently upon the plot which has to interrelate the three worlds of the novel and also display ironically the inability of the characters to handle events. The author, it appears, is unwilling to commit himself finally on the precise relationship between inner and outer, between Ezeulu's need for power and the god he worships, between Winterbottom's aggressiveness and the rituals of power he practices. The uncertainty we are left in is the price we have to pay for the fine rendering of the several social worlds of the novel where ritual and convention differentiate and also unify the lives of the characters.

CHAPTER 5

A Man of the People

THE careers of Achebe's two strongminded heroes, Okonkwo and Ezeulu, covered the period just before and after the arrival of the Europeans among the Ibo. The careers of his two alienated modern heroes fall on either side of political independence in West Africa: Obi's schizophrenia reached its climax in the 1950's before independence when the influence of Africa and Europe seemed nicely poised, while the narrator of Achebe's next novel, *A Man of the People* (1966), views with distaste an unnamed, newly independent West African country in the 1960's where Africanization is the order of the day. All four are political novels, but when we group them in this way it is apparent that the two set in the earlier period describe attacks, both internal and external, upon the traditional Ibo way of life, while the two later novels, far more pessimistic in tone, diagnose the aftereffects of this conflict in the modern state.

In *No Longer at Ease*, the conflict was embodied rather diagrammatically in the makeup of the hybrid hero; when the two cultures he attempts to reconcile are shown to be contradictory, he succumbs halfheartedly. In *A Man of the People*, the conflict between different values is delineated by means of a central dramatic relationship far more vital and convincing than the dismemberment of Obi Okonkwo. The main characters are Chief Nanga, the minister of culture, and the schoolmaster, Odili Samalu. The two men occupy opposite ends of the political spectrum, and their relationship defines the basic problems of political morality. Odili has a fastidious, theoretical view of public morality derived from his European type of education, and we find him at the beginning of the novel thoroughly disillusioned with political affairs in his own country. He has rejected all local, political allegiances— "primitive loyalties" he calls them—and refuses to acknowledge that these might have value for other people. From his detached, alienated point of view he condemns the corruption he sees around him and remains aloof.

Nanga, the politician in power, occupies the other end of the political spectrum. He is a realist whose morality is one of survival. Unconcerned with the theory of politics, he has an instinctive grasp of what the electorate want. They want, he says, their share of the national cake. But he is not simply "a man of the people" in this cynical sense. He also has a genuine sympathy and rapport with the people he represents, and this comes across to the reader as an infectious bonhomie which it is difficult to resist. He does not discount the people's primitive loyalties; even as he exploits them he remains sensitive to their demands, so that there is an ironical half-truth in his assertion that he represents government "of the people, by the people, for the people."

The relationship between these two men, a strange blend of fascination and repulsion, dramatically and colorfully defines the problems of public and private morality in a society which has lost sight of its past and looks to the future for material rewards. The decline in public values is implicit in the incident of Josiah and the blind beggar. Josiah is a village trader who makes several appearances in the course of the novel. On one occasion he steals a blind beggar's walking stick "to make," as one old woman says, "a medicine to turn us into blind buyers of his wares." This unscrupulous act is too much for the villagers who boycott his store: "Within one week Josiah was ruined; no man, woman, or child went near his shop" (ix). In the village there is still some kind of social code which can mobilize the people for effective action. The phrase the villagers use to justify their action—"Josiah has taken away enough for the owner to notice"—takes us back to the communities of Umuofia and Umuaro resisting the first erosions of their traditional values. But by now the erosion is so far advanced that this communal village act is only a vestigial remnant of a social ethic we have witnessed in its full vigor. The incident comes as a revelation to the alienated Odili:

I thought much afterwards about that proverb, about the man taking things away until the owner at last notices. In the mouth of our people there was no greater condemnation. It was not just a simple question of a man's cup being full. A man's cup might be full and none be the wiser. But here the owner knew, and the owner, I discovered, is the will of the whole people. (ix)

The proverb runs through the novel like a refrain reminding us of what has been lost and asserting that the turgid problems of the present cannot be solved by any recourse to the general will.

The uncertainties of the first-person method of narration which Achebe uses in this novel for the first time reflects this absence of stable values. We have come a long way from the wise ancestral voice of *Things Fall Apart*. The novel is narrated from the fastidious point of view of the schoolteacher Odili who is, of course, intent on justifying his own values and actions at the same time as he maligns the motives of Nanga. This is a new departure for Achebe, but with the earlier novels in mind it comes as no surprise. The most persistent feature of those works was the juxtaposition and conflict of different systems of value, African and European, either in the mind of the hero as in *No Longer at Ease* or in the dramatic confrontation of colonialists and villagers in *Arrow of God*. Now the conflict of values is reflected in the technique of narration. In *A Man of the People*, the dialectic is pressed upon us continuously as we seek to balance the unreliable narrator against the flawed title-hero he is seeking to denigrate. We are required to examine the object and the point of view from which it is presented, making the adjustments necessary to counteract the double refraction of malice and self-justification. In the last resort, subject and object are inseparable; there is no detached standpoint from which we may isolate and assess the characters with confidence. This is the relativity of experience which the unreliability of first-person narration represents. The only guidance is to be found in the later, more mature comments of the narrator as he looks back at his earlier actions.

I *The Protagonists*

The first few chapters of the novel present the relationship between the two main characters before they become openly hostile. Here they explore each other's character, and Achebe begins to suggest in each case how political ideology is inseparable from personal psychology.

The novel opens in 1964 with the official visit of Chief the Honourable M.A. Nanga M.P. to Anata Grammar School where he himself used to be a teacher and where the narrator Odili is now teaching. The visit is seen through the skeptical eyes of Odili, who has been thoroughly disillusioned by the political events of the

last few years. His disillusionment embraces both the politicians
and the electorate who have cynically entered into a conspiracy of
self-interest. The politicians safeguard their own interests by providing their local supporters with a slice of "the national cake."
Things have finally fallen apart in this general moral decay:

As I stood in one corner of that vast tumult waiting for the arrival of
the Minister I felt intense bitterness welling up in my mouth. Here
were silly, ignorant villagers dancing themselves lame and waiting to
blow off their gun-powder in honour of one of those who had started
the country off down the slopes of inflation. I wished for a miracle, for
a voice of thunder, to hush this ridiculous festival and tell the poor
contemptible people one or two truths. But of course it would be quite
useless. They were not only ignorant but cynical. Tell them that this
man had used his position to enrich himself and they would ask you—
as my father did—if you thought that a sensible man would spit out
the juicy morsel that good fortune placed in his mouth. (i)

But the bustle and vitality of the scene, with the women dancing,
the hunter's guild in full regalia, and old "Grammar-phone"
herself singing, make themselves heard above the narrator's disapproval. His concern over economic inflation and political immorality pale into academic insignificance. Here is the tribal chief
making a triumphal return and this surely merits a local celebra-
tion. And yet, for Odili it is precisely the success of this attempt to
turn a national politician into a clan leader which causes dismay
and disillusionment. It means that national interest will always
come second, that government resolves itself into a squabble of
local loyalties and interests. The singing, the hunter's guild, the
dancing which he dislikes, the minister's "ever-present fan of animal skin which they said fanned away all evil designs and shafts
of malevolence thrown at him by the wicked"—all these are symbols, for Odili, of the vitiation of government by local allegiances.
   Consequently, Odili has opted out of politics, and he describes
in a flashback how this occurred. His adolescent hero worship of
Nanga, dating from 1948, was finally destroyed by the 1960 economic crisis in which his hero first came to the public notice. On
his first and last visit to Parliament he witnessed the political as-
sassination of the minister of finance, "a first-rate economist with a
Ph.D. in public finance," by a government unwilling to face up to
the stringent and unpopular measures he proposed. Nanga was

well to the fore in hounding and condemning. But what was so disillusioning to Odili, an undergraduate at the time, was the form taken by the discrediting of the minister of finance. The minister and his colleagues were attacked for being un-African, "decadent stooges versed in text-book economics and aping the white man's mannerisms and way of speaking." The quotation from the official party organ continues: "We are proud to be Africans. Our true leaders are not those intoxicated with their Oxford, Cambridge or Harvard degrees but those who speak the language of the people. Away with the damnable and expensive university education which only alienates an African from his rich and ancient culture and puts him above his people . . ." (i). If it is a choice between parliamentary democracy with all its European associations and self-interest masquerading as Africanization, then Odili prefers the former. But then the episode of Josiah and the blind man's stick again raises the question: What if there is no such thing as a national consciousness but only a conglomeration of clan or village loyalties? In this case, Odili's European political concepts could be irrelevant, even dangerous, and he, like the minister of finance, could be labeled a member of "the hybrid class of Western educated and snobbish intellectuals who will not hesitate to sell their mothers for a mess of pottage" (i). And Odili *is* a hybrid who views with distaste not only the corruption but many other features of his society. His ambition is to take a postgraduate diploma in London and be accepted in a European society.

At this point in his analysis, Achebe moves almost imperceptibly from the political to the personal. Odili's political views are shown to be inseparable from his character. The personality which adheres to these highminded yet disillusioned concepts is by nature coldblooded, egocentric, and alienated. The narrator, of course, does not describe himself in these terms. As far as he is concerned he is simply unwilling "to lick any Big Man's boots": "In fact one reason why I took this teaching job in a bush, private school instead of a smart civil service job in the city with car, free housing, etc., was to give myself a certain amount of autonomy" (ii). Autonomy in the political sphere may be admirable but when it is transferred to the local community and to personal relations it becomes alienation and selfishness.

He exemplifies his personal selfishness most clearly in his relations with his girl friend, Elsie. She is his proudest trophy, the biggest boost to his self-esteem. He admits that he is not usually lucky with women, but with her it was different: "she was, and for that matter still is, the only girl I met and slept with the same day—in fact within an hour" (ii). Elsie's main attraction, apart from providing proof of his sexual powers, is her undemanding availability: "I can't pretend that I ever thought of marriage. . . . Elsie was such a beautiful, happy girl and she made no demands whatever" (ii). This is what autonomy becomes in the world of Odili's private affairs.

Achebe has not yet completed the search for the private origins of his narrator's public values. As in *No Longer at Ease* he sends his character on an unwilling visit to his home village of Urua, to see his estranged father whom he despises. The two major clues uncovered here are that his mother died at his birth and that his father was a district interpreter. Both circumstances fostered the loneliness and alienation of the sensitive child. He was known as the "bad child that crunched his mother's skull":

Of course as soon as I grew old enough to understand a few simple proverbs I realized that I should have died and let my mother live. Whenever my people go to console a woman whose baby had died at birth or soon after, they always tell her to dry her eyes because it is better the water is spilled than the pot broken. The idea being that a sound pot can always return to the stream. (iii)

The second clue means that Odili was the son of the most unpopular man in the district. In the days of his childhood, "the D.O. was like the Supreme Deity, and the Interpreter the principal minor god who carried prayers and sacrifice to Him. . . . So Interpreters in those days were powerful, very rich, widely known and hated" (iii). In the manner of a Dickensian hero Odili's alienation dates from the moment of his birth, and he grows up in a world full of enemies.

We can now see the paradoxical relationship between his public values and character. Odili's political views can be so immaculately highminded, so uncontaminated by personal allegiance because his detachment from his fellow human beings is virtually total. It is through this contradictory, dissatisfied mind that the events of the novel are mediated.

Nanga's values are equally ambiguous. At first sight he is a political opportunist whose only concerns are survival and self-interest. Without detachment of any kind he has no concept of political morality or of the national good. As the narrator realizes, his concerns are local and immediate: "people like Chief Nanga don't care two hoots about the outside world. He is concerned with the inside world, with how to retain his hold on his constituency and there he is adept" (ii). Nanga has an instinctive grasp of how to do this, and he is prepared to call to his assistance bribery, corruption, and intimidation.

Political opportunism of this kind controls the public world of the novel. Unlike the village where the unscrupulous Josiah is quickly and effectively outlawed, the country as a whole has no kind of political morality by which to judge and condemn a Nanga. And so he and his ministerial colleagues pursue their various forms of self-interest with an occasional return to the constituency with promises of a slice of the national cake for everyone. The results of this are the recurrent political and economic crises with which the events of the novel are punctuated. Certainly in this political sphere Odili's disillusionment seems the only response.

In the context of the local scene, however, Nanga assumes a vitality and stature which are very compelling. As we see him speaking and joking with the villagers in pidgin English, sharing their values and expressing their political hopes, he becomes a man of the people in a less ironical sense. In contrast, the narrator appears debilitated by superciliousness. One is forced to look again at the earlier demotic denunciation of the "hybrid class of Western-educated" Africans and wonder if there is some truth in the charges leveled against them. Nanga, in contrast, does speak "the language of the people" and has not undergone "a university education which only alienates an African from his rich and ancient culture and puts him above his people." The alienated Odili and his friend sneer at Nanga's parochialism: "Just think of such a cultureless man going abroad and calling himself Minister of Culture. Ridiculous. This is why the outside world laughs at us" (ii). But in his own vulgar, vital way he possesses more culture than the disinherited class to which they belong. His culture manifests itself spontaneously in gesture, dance, language, and dress. It is through these that Nanga comes to life, for his culture is inseparable from his electric personality. This is the quality which enables him to adapt his new role, which the villagers only dimly understand, to their traditional needs, and although, as we have seen, this constitutes the main threat to any kind of parliamentary democracy, the continuity preserved by such an adaptation carries with it meaning and vitality. Nanga is welcomed back to his constituency like a chief who will always safeguard the interests of his people:

As soon as the Minister's Cadillac arrived at the head of a long motorcade the hunters dashed this way and that and let off their last shots, throwing their guns about with frightening freedom. The dancers capered and stamped, filling the dry-season air with dust. Not even Grammar-phone's voice could now be heard over the tumult. The Minister stepped out wearing damask and gold chains and acknowledging cheers with his ever-present fan of animal skin. . . . (i)

It is a triumph of style unaffected by the sneers of the narrator.

Nanga becomes increasingly attractive as we move from his doubtful political ideals to his personality. The reverse was true of the narrator who consequently has some difficulty in diagnosing the cause of Nanga's success. Eventually he too begins to succumb to the infectious charm: "The man was still as handsome and youthful-looking as ever—there was no doubt about that. . . . The Minister had a jovial word for everyone. You could never think—looking at him now—that his smile was anything but genuine. It seemed bloody-minded to be sceptical" (i). Odili is taken further aback when the Minister recognizes him from his schooldays, embraces him, and offers assistance. For Nanga, this is where values and ideals come alive. Now Odili's comment on current political corruption—"A common saying in the country after Independence was that it didn't matter *what* you knew but *who* you knew"—seems far less sinister in its implications. Nanga works through local allegiances and, whatever the shortcomings, he does speak for the people he represents.

These are the two main characters. When the necessary adjustments have been made to counter the narrator's prejudices, it is clear that there is a symmetry in their juxtaposition. At the public level, the self-interest of the political opportunist is contrasted with the ideals of the disillusioned narrator; at the private level, the opportunist's warmth and vitality are contrasted with the alienation and selfishness of the idealist. The choice seems to be between idealism protected by irony and detachment, and involvement denied a wider view of political realities. The rest of the novel plots the implications, the ironies, and the resolution of this choice.

II *At Chief Nanga's Feet*

At the first meeting of the two men their characteristic styles are contrasted. The narrator is disapproving and on the defensive. "I held out my hand somewhat stiffly. I did not have the slightest fear that he might remember me and had no intention of reminding him" (i). When Nanga does recognize him his need for affection and popularity makes him secretly delighted. Already he begins to wonder if he "had been applying to politics stringent standards that didn't belong to it." Nanga, free from such hesitations, slaps the narrator on the back and chides him for not having sought his help: "Don't you know that minister means servant? Busy or no busy he must see his master." He quickly invites him to stay at his house in the capital, Bori, and offers assistance with his scholarship to England. Then, without a pause, he delivers a speech to this Anata "family reunion" which even Odili acknowledges "sounded spontaneous and was most effective." Then the natural impresario mixes with the people: "Outside, the dancers had all come alive again and the hunters—their last powder gone—were tamely waiting for the promised palm-wine. The Minister danced a few dignified steps to the music of each group and stuck red pound notes on the perspiring faces of the best dancers" (i). Watched by the detached, critical narrator, the extrovert man of power moves with a political instinct that has become second nature. Achebe manages the contrast excellently.

His most effective means of contrast is the speech of the two men. The sophisticated narrator employs correct English usage to formulate his disapproval of Nanga and the society he represents; the man of the people uses West Coast pidgin of varying intensity. The conclusion of the first encounter between the two men suggests what a fine expression of character is provided by Nanga's vigorous colloquialisms.

Later on in the Proprietor's Lodge I said to the Minister: "You must have spent a fortune today."

He smiled at the glass of cold beer in his hand and said:

"You call this spend? You never see some thing, my brother. I no de

keep anini for myself, na so so troway. If some person come to you and
say "I wan' make you Minister" make you run like blazes comot. Na
true word I tell you. To God who made me." He showed the tip of his
tongue to the sky to confirm the oath. "Minister de sweet for eye but
too much katakata de for inside. Believe me yours sincerely."
"Big man, big palaver," said the one-eyed man. (i)

In *Things Fall Apart* and *Arrow of God* pidgin was used sparingly
to signify the meretriciousness of the forces seeking to erode traditional Ibo values which were expressed through a simple yet dignified English. By the time of *A Man of the People* there has been
a reversal. When Nanga employs pidgin in this flexible, colorful
way we are compelled to see it as an African means of combating
European, cosmopolitan values. Certainly in this case the language, the exaggerations, the gestures, all disturb Odili's measured, self-conscious narration. They dramatize the vital force of a
man who draws his strength, however unscrupulously, from the
people and who is unconcerned about the disapproval of the
squeamish intellectuals. The two schoolteachers make subtly
waspish comments in an attempt to deflate the minister: when
these are ignored in the general adulation, they turn their irony
against each other.

Despite his criticisms, Odili accepts Nanga's invitation and his
few days spent in the minister's household form a crucial stage in
his political education: "sitting at Chief Nanga's feet I received
enlightenment; many things began to crystallize out of the mist—
some of the emergent forms were not nearly as ugly as I had suspected but many seemed much worse. However, I was not making these judgements at the time, or not strongly anyhow" (iv).
The final comment reminds us that the novel as a whole is arranged in retrospect by the mature narrator who has had time to
digest the significance of the events he is describing. In the uncertain world of the first-person novel the narrator's comments upon
his earlier self exercise the chief control on the trajectory of the
novel as a whole. Achebe is not consistently successful in his manipulation of this fictional device. At times the distinction between
the narrator and his earlier self is blurred and with it the nature of
his education. Then suddenly the author seems to remember the
important function of this narrative strategy and become excessively explicit:

The difficulty in writing this kind of story is that the writer is armed with all kinds of hindsight which he didn't have when the original events were happening. When he introduces a character like Elsie for instance, he already has at the back of his mind a total picture of her; her entrance, her act and her exit. And this tends to colour even the first words he writes. I can only hope that being aware of this danger I have successfully kept it at bay. As far as is humanly possible I shall try not to jump ahead of my story. (ii)

This has no apparent dramatic function; it simply reminds the reader that this is a novel narrated in retrospect by one of the characters. This absence of clear focus occasionally blurs the significance of events in the Nanga household.

At first, the narrator experiences admiration and envy as he sees the minister at close quarters and his earlier detachment disappears. "All I can say is that on that first night there was no room in my mind for criticism. I was simply hypnotized by the luxury of the great suite assigned to me . . . I had to confess that if I were at that moment made a minister I would be most anxious to remain one for ever. And maybe I should have thanked God that I wasn't" (iii). Odili has come under the influence of the Nanga charisma so that he now begins to explain sympathetically the temptations of the men of power:

A man who has just come in from the rain and dried his body and put on dry clothes is more reluctant to go out again than another who has been indoors all the time. The trouble with our new nation—as I saw it then lying on that bed—was that none of us had been indoors long enough to be able to say "to hell with it." We had all been in the rain together until yesterday. Then a handful of us—the smart and the lucky and hardly ever the best—had scrambled for the one shelter our former rulers left, and had taken it over and barricaded themselves in. (iii)

The shift from the first- to the third-person pronoun in the final sentence suggests an ambiguity in the narrator's loyalties. But clearly his disapproval of the politicians is now tempered by a closer insight into the temptations and problems of power.

Life at the Nangas' during the next few days further undermines Odili's clear-cut views. His earlier ideals begin to look rather attenuated in the midst of the whirl of activity created by Nanga's

indefatigable energy. He wonders if it is unrealistic "to bring into
politics niceties and delicate refinements that belonged elsewhere"
(i). And yet this suggests that the world of ideals and the world
of power are quite unrelated. Is it not possible, then, to pass judgment on the political world? Odili is discovering the paradox that
detachment implies lack of understanding, while involvement
precludes objectivity. A series of conversations juxtaposed in an
apparently arbitrary manner explore this predicament and question not only any simple judgment of Nanga but also the reliabil-
ity of the novel's narrator.

The paradox of detachment and involvement is defined by
means of the relations between Africans and Europeans. The two
cultures meet at Nanga's house, and the relativity of values becomes the theme which links the separate incidents. First, there is
the cook who comes for a job and can only prepare European
food. His wife cooks the African food he eats: "How man wey
get family go begin enter kitchen for make bitterleaf and egusi?
Unless if the man no get shame" (iv). He doesn't get the job
because Nanga prefers African food, but the narrator sympathizes
with him amid the general amusement: "But I must say the fellow
had a point. As long as a man confined himself to preparing foreign concoctions he could still maintain the comfortable illusion
that he wasn't really doing such an unmanly thing as cooking"
(iv). This is a shrewd but unwitting comment on Odili himself
and the stratagems he employs to maintain similar illusions, both
political and personal.

The second variation on this theme is more overt. After Nanga's
departure, the guests are discussing a recent piece of sculpture,
the wooden figure of a god carved by a local artist. An Englishman is convinced that it is "bad or un-African": he has seen an old
woman shaking her fist at it in a rage in the public square. She is
in a position to judge, not because she has been trained in European art schools, but because she "most probably worshipped this
very god herself." At this point, Odili experiences his "flash of insight":

"Did you say she was shaking her fist?" I asked. "In that case you
got her meaning all wrong. Shaking the fist in our society is a sign of
great honour and respect; it means that you attribute power to the
person or object." Which of course is quite true. And if I may digress

a little, I have since this incident, come up against another critic who
committed a crime in my view because he transferred to an alien culture the same meanings and interpretation that his own people attach
to certain gestures and facial expression. (v)

The cook was seeking to preserve his self-respect by adopting superior European customs; the Englishman shows his superiority
by adopting what he thinks are African criteria. The narrator's
comment shows the difficulty of attributing correct motives in an
alien culture and presumably alerts him to the simplifications of
his own European-style assessment of Nanga.
    When the other guests leave, Odili is alone with the American
hostess, Jean. They dance a highlife together, and we are treated
to a further variation of cultural misunderstanding:

I must say she had learnt to do the highlife well except that like many
another foreign enthusiast of African rhythm she tended to overdo the
waist wiggle. I don't say I found it unpleasant—quite on the contrary;
I only make a general point, which I think is interesting. It all goes
back to what others have come to associate us with. And let it be said
that we are not entirely blameless in this. I remember how we were
outraged at the University to see a film of breast-throwing, hip-jerking,
young women which a neighbouring African state had made and was
showing abroad as an African ballet. Jean probably saw it in America.
(v)

Not only do we find it necessary to impose stereotypes on other
people; they in turn strengthen the stereotypes by acting as we
want them to act. An additional irony in this case is that Jean's
husband, Odili tells us, is away on business, "advising our government on how to improve its public image in America."
    The permutations multiply. Jean wrongfully attributes sexual
motives to Odili which he is delighted to acknowledge, and next
we see them in bed together. But the chapter ends in complete
misunderstanding. Jean takes him on a tour of the city as she
drives him home: "She certainly knew the city well, from the fresh-
smelling modern waterfront to the stinking, maggoty interior."
Despite their intimacy, Odili begins to mistrust her motives: Was
it simply for curiosity's sake or was there "some secret reason, like
wanting me to feel ashamed about my country's capital city?" He
laughs uneasily at the signs of corruption and inequality in Bori,

signs which he had enjoyed with unconcealed pleasure when
alone in the previous chapter. Now his suspicions and pride are
aroused: "Who the hell did she think she was to laugh so self-
righteously. Wasn't there enough in her own country to keep her
laughing all her days? Or crying if she preferred it?" (v). He sup-
presses his anger, and the episode ends uneasily without an open
quarrel.

This sequence of incidents has two effects on the narrator. He
now understands the difficulty of trying to interpret or judge any
alien culture or area of experience in which one has not partici-
pated directly and intimately. And secondly, as he has sought to
correct the most blatant errors of the Europeans, Odili has become increasingly protective and defensive about his own African
society. He is beginning to see his earlier detachment for what it
was: a means of avoiding contamination in a society of which he
is necessarily a part. It should be added that the reader has at
times some difficulty in determining the precise attitude of the
author toward his narrator. On some occasions as the theme of
this section of the novel is developed Odili seems to speak directly
for the author. He introduces his "flash of insight" over the piece
of sculpture for example by saying, "I made what I still think was
a most valid and timely intervention." In other words, the narrator
agrees with his earlier self, and the author presumably agrees with
both. The reason could be, of course, that Odili's education is
really getting under way; the more plausible explanation is that
the author wants to make a point about cultural relativism and
that for the moment the dramatic function of the first-person
method of narration is in abeyance. The trouble is we are not
certain. The focus which the character of the narrator should provide is not sufficiently clear.

III *Hostilities*

Odili's growing sympathy for Nanga and uncertainty about his
own loyalties end abruptly when he takes his girl friend Elsie to
stay at Nanga's house. Characteristically, he has given the minister the impression that she is "simply a good-time girl": "I suppose
what happened was that Chief Nanga and I having already
swopped many tales of conquest I felt somehow compelled to
speak in derogatory terms about women in general" (vi). In the
absence of his wife, Nanga doesn't wait for niceties of definition

to be cleared up. He is in Elsie's bedroom before the narrator
"could muster up sufficient bravado to step into the sitting-room
and up the stairs." Then, when he hears "as from a great distance
Elsie deliriously screaming my name," Odili suffers a crisis of inertia:

I find it difficult in retrospect to understand my inaction at that moment. A sort of paralysis had spread over my limbs, while an intense
pressure was building up inside my chest. But before it reached raging
point I felt it siphoned off, leaving me empty inside and out. I trudged
up the stairs in the incredible delusion that Elsie was calling on me to
come and save her from her ravisher. But when I got to the door a
strong revulsion and hatred swept over me and I turned sharply away
and went down the stairs for the last time.

Elsie's desperate screams become ambiguous when we recall that
"She was one of those girls who send out loud cries in the heat of
the thing" (ii). What she usually calls out is the name of her previous lover. Odili no longer finds it amusing.

Humiliated and angered, he leaves the house in the small hours
of the morning, but despite what has happened he retains his previous cold detachment:

As dawn came my head began to clear a little and I saw Bori stirring.
I met a night-soil man carrying his bucket of ordure on top of a bat-
tered felt hat drawn down to hood his upper face while his nose and
mouth were masked with a piece of black cloth like a gangster. I saw
beggars sleeping under the eaves of luxurious department stores and a
lunatic sitting wide awake by the basket of garbage he called his possession. The first red buses running empty passed me and I watched the
street lights go off finally around six. I drank in all these details with
the early morning air.

The politician has acted decisively, the fastidious intellectual has
been outmaneuvered and now observes exactly the details of the
scene. This is the moment of clearsighted disenchantment; after
the period of disdain and the period of sympathy with Nanga,
comes this detachment. The later Odili comments in retrospect:
"It was strange perhaps that a man who had so much on his mind
should find time to pay attention to these small, inconsequential
things; it was like the man in the proverb who was carrying the

carcass of an elephant on his head and searching with his toes for a grasshopper. But that was how it happened. It seems that no thought—no matter how great—had the power to exclude all others." He now returns to confront and denounce Nanga in a characteristically halfhearted way: " 'What a country?' I said. 'You call yourself Minister of Culture? God help us.' And I spat; not a full spit but a token, albeit unmistakable, one" (vii). Nanga, understandably baffled by his reaction, offers Odili other girls in exchange for Elsie, but the break has now occurred and open hostility continues for the rest of the novel.

This blow to his pride at last forces Odili to act, but not immediately. At first he seeks to rationalize the insult in what the narrator now realizes was an unworthy manner: "But I suppose it was possible (judging by the way things finally worked themselves out) that these weak and trivial thoughts might have been a sort of smoke-screen behind which, unknown to me, weighty decisions were taking shape" (viii). The decision, when it comes, is uncharacteristically violent: "What mattered was that a man had treated me as no man had a right to treat another—not even if he was master and the other slave; and my manhood required that I make him pay for his insult in full measure." He will "seek out Nanga's intended parlour-wife and give her the works, good and proper." The "parlour-wife" who is to supplement Nanga's legal wife is Edna, in whom Odili has been showing considerable interest since the opening episode of the novel. Now this interest turns into a vicious form of revenge. Nanga is no longer simply a politician whose values he despises; he is a rival who has taken Elsie by force. As we have been led to expect, Odili is capable of acting viciously and selfishly on the level of personal relations.

Unexpectedly he gains support for his revenge from his friend in Bori, Max, who is about to form a new political party, the Common People's Convention, to rescue their "hard-won freedom" from corruption. Odili agrees to become a founder member: "It would add a second string to my bow when I came to deal with Nanga" (viii). From here to the end of the novel the narrator's public concern and his private vendetta intermingle in a double campaign against the minister. Apparently it is a failure at both levels, but it brings self-knowledge to the narrator.

Both the planned seduction of Edna and the political campaign begin rather unsteadily. Odili first insults Edna's father, who is delighted with the prospect of Nanga as a son-in-law, while in the political sphere the conspirators shed nostalgic tears over Max's piece of poetry written "during the intoxicating months of high hope soon after Independence." When they turn to political action one of the first things Odili discovers is that their new party is backed by a junior minister in the present government. He wonders why he does not resign: " 'Resign?' laughed Max. 'Where do you think you are—Britain or something?' " (viii). Odili does not want to appear naïve, and yet his early idealism persists: "I would have thought it was better to start our new party clean, with a different kind of philosophy." But now he begins to realize that philosophies and principles have to fight desperately for survival. At this point occurs the village boycott of Josiah and the episode underlines the fact that he is now trying to operate in a political world devoid of any accepted code of conduct.

The uncovering of the trade scandal gives a strong fillip to both of the narrator's campaigns:

The country was on the verge of chaos. The Trade Unions and the Civil Service Union made loud noises and gave notice of nation-wide strikes. The shops closed for fear of looting. The Governor-General according to rumour called on the Prime-Minister to resign which he finally got round to doing three weeks later. (x)

He now returns to the attack with Edna and also, to everyone's amusement, announces that he is going to contest Nanga's seat at the imminent election. Ominously at this point the outlawed Josiah comes to offer his services in the election campaign. He sees their positions as analogous: they are both outlaws. The irony is, of course, that Josiah is outlawed because of his low principles in the village, Odili because of his excessively high principles in national politics. Odili turns him down.

Even now Odili makes very little headway against Nanga's private and public popularity. At the inaugural meeting of his constituency Nanga's hirelings make a fool of him to the great delight of the crowd, and then he is threatened by Edna's father first with a matchet and then with an allegory: "My in-law is like a bull, and your challenge is like the challenge of a tick to a bull. The tick fills its belly with blood from the back of the bull and the bull doesn't even know it's there" (x). In addition and in quick succession, he is sacked by his headmaster, abused by Mrs. Nanga, and intimidated by Nanga's supporters. But this low point in his fortunes leads to what is so far his most important piece of self-discovery. He begins to see that the danger and insults he has been prepared to undergo in his pursuit of Edna are significant: "And at that very moment I was suddenly confronted by a fact I had been dodging for some time. I knew then that I wanted Edna now (if not all along) for her own sake first and foremost and only very remotely as part of a general scheme of revenge" (xi). Beginning to see through the stratagems of his alienated self, Odili can now move away from his defensive posture and acknowledge his love for Edna.

He then turns to his political motives: "Having got that far in my self-analysis I had to ask myself one question. How important was my political activity in its own right?" The answer to this isn't clear: "It was difficult to say; things seemed so mixed up; my revenge, my new political ambition and the girl. And perhaps it was just as well that my motives should entangle and reinforce one another." But in his self-analysis Odili is clearly beginning the disentanglement. His love for Edna has already been separated from his desire for revenge, and now his political ambition is at last recognized as a genuine desire to destroy Nanga and the corruption he represents. "Although I had little hope of winning Chief Nanga's seat, it was necessary nonetheless to fight and expose him as much as possible. . . ." Then perhaps some kind of rudimentary political morality might revive and condemn him. Odili expreses this hope in terms of the proverb which is repeated so many times: "and maybe someone would get up and say: 'No, Nanga has taken more than the owner could ignore!' But it was no more than a hope" (xi). Odili has thus begun to disentangle and purify his motives. As he does so the two halves of his character move closer toward a reconciliation. The private self emerges from its defensive cocoon and declares itself, while the public self comes down from its impossibly high and disillusioned standards and seeks to achieve the possible.

As he sets off on his political campaign, Odili looks back on the earlier stages of his career and sees them as a reflection of the changes in the country as a whole. "I could not help thinking also of the quick transformations that were such a feature of our country, and in particular of the changes of attitude in my own self."

He recalls that on entering university his one ambition was to become "a full member of the privileged class whose symbol was the car." After an "intellectual crisis" he rejected this in favor of the disillusioned idealism he displays at the beginning of the novel: "Many of us vowed then never to be corrupted by bourgeois privileges of which the car was the most visible symbol in our country." Now as he drives off in his new car acquired through party funds he scrutinizes his present position: "And now here was I in this marvellous little affair eating the hills like yam—as Edna would have said. I hoped I was safe; for a man who avoids danger for years and then gets killed in the end has wasted his care." This does not represent a reversion to his earlier materialism, but rather a difficult attempt to synthesize the two earlier stages of his development. He stands a far better chance of balancing involvement with some kind of political idealism now that he has disentangled the complex motives controlling his actions.

It soon becomes apparent that it is going to be difficult to keep his idealism untarnished during the campaign. First, he must have bodyguards. Then reluctantly he agrees to their carrying weapons. Finally he has to provide money for bribing important officials. His objections are answered very firmly by his guard: "Look my frien I done tell you say if you no wan serious for this business make you go rest for house. I done see say you want play too much gentleman for this matter . . . Dem tell you say na gentlemanity de give other people minister . . . ?" (xi). His father too, convinced as he is "that the mainspring of political action was material gain," expects some material advantage from his son's new career. He imagines the big opportunity has come when Nanga, who wants to be re-elected unopposed, appears with £250 to bribe his son to stand down: "Take your money and take your scholarship and go and learn more book; the country needs experts like you. And leave the dirty game of politics to us who know how to play it . . ." (xi).

These are the contradictory pressures at work on Odili; the one seeking to drag him into the political rat race and make him succumb to the forces which have molded a Nanga, the other trying to push him back into his earlier, detached disillusionment. He rejects Nanga's offer with scorn ("I see the fear in your eyes") and presses on with his campaign. His only cause for concern is that Max has accepted a similar offer. Max confirms this and reassures

the disturbed Odili by saying that he does not consider it legally
binding: "Now you tell me how you propose to fight such a dirty
war without soiling your hands a little" (xii). Odili stands firm.
Involvement requires realistic political methods but not capitulation to the national cake ethic and all it stands for:

The real point surely was that Max's action had jeopardized our moral
position, our ability to inspire that kind of terror which I had seen so
clearly in Nanga's eyes despite all his grandiloquent bluff, and which
in the end was our society's only hope of salvation. (xii)

There is, however, enough of the self-opinionated earlier Odili left
for him to feel rather hurt that Max's bribe was larger than the
sum he was offered.

This political setback and his subsequent rebuff by Edna make
him realize sadly that Nanga had won the second round in his
double campaign to win "a beautiful life with Edna and a new era
of cleanliness in the politics of our country." Perhaps he should
abandon his political plans along with Edna who had helped to
crystallize them. Then comes Odili's final flash of insight. He will
not succumb but make one final attempt to realize his ideals in
action.

The knowledge that Chief Nanga had won the first two rounds and,
on the present showing, would win the third and last far from suggesting thoughts of surrender to my mind served to harden my resolution.
What I had to accomplish became more than another squabble for
political office; it rose suddenly to the heights of symbolic action, a
shining, monumental gesture untainted by hopes of success or reward.
(xii)

The gesture when it is made is neither shining nor monumental
but certainly symbolic of a changed Odili who has through his
own chastening experiences learned something of the political realities he scorned at the opening of the novel.

IV A Shining, Monumental Gesture

The final events of the novel begin with the capitulation of the
Urua constituency to Nanga's chicanery. The village is helpless in
the sphere of national politics: it elects but does not control.

Two nights later we heard the sound of the Crier's gong. His message was unusual. In the past the Crier had summoned the village to a meeting to deliberate over a weighty question, or else to some accustomed communal labour. His business was to serve notice of something that was to happen. But this night he did something new: he announced a decision already taken. (xiii)

Odili's question—"if the whole people had taken the decision why were they now being told of it?"—points to the perversion of the communal ethic which, thanks to the Josiah episode, Odili has come to understand. Unlike the traditional communities of Umuofia and Umuaro, this constituency is at the mercy of the politicians who claim to represent it, and Odili feels sympathy rather than anger: "In the afternoon the radio, our national Crier, took up the message, amplified it and gave it in four languages including English. . . . I couldn't say I blamed my village people for recoiling from the role of sacrificial ram. Why should they lose their chance of getting good, clean water, their share of the national cake?" (xiii).

This new kind of resigned understanding is not restricted to Odili's public values. His father unexpectedly supports him at this juncture and he begins to wonder if here too he has been rash and shortsighted in his judgments: "I realized that I had never really been close enough to my father to understand him. I had built up a private picture of him from unconnected scraps of evidence." He wonders if he has got "everything terribly, lopsidedly wrong," but postpones for the moment any new assessment.

The climax of the novel, Odili's opportunity for the grand gesture, occurs at Nanga's inaugural campaign meeting. There he sees Nanga in full regalia, his wife, and Edna, and there he experiences again the desire to denounce this man of the people. The novel has come full circle, and we are back at the opening episode with the narrator's angry fantasy:

What would happen if I were to push my way to the front and up the palm-leaf-festooned dais, wrench the microphone from the greasy hands of that blabbing buffoon and tell the whole people—this vast contemptible crowd—that the great man they had come to hear with their drums and dancing was an Honourable Thief. But of course they knew that already. (xiii)

As he is exercising his fancy in this way, he is spotted, despite his disguise, by Josiah now an ally of Nanga. He tries to escape but as he hears the cry "Stop thief!" he pauses: "I wanted to know who called me a thief." Nanga summons him to the dais and, surrounded by his supporters, ridicules the narrator whom he now sees as a ludicrous rather than a dangerous figure. Odili, his fastidious detachment a thing of the past, reacts unexpectedly: "My panic had now left me entirely and in its place I found a rock-cold fearlessness that I had never before felt in my heart. I watched Nanga, microphone in one hand, reeling about the dais in drunken jubilation. I seemed to see him from a superior, impregnable position." At this final confrontation, they each recognize the other with complete clarity as the antagonist.

Nanga begins with his own account of the events of the novel: "This is the boy who is thrusting his finger into my eye. He came to my house in Bori, ate my food, drank my water and my wine and instead of saying thank you to me he set about plotting how to drive me out and take over my house." From the point of view of someone with Nanga's values this and what follows is a substantially true version of events. Our view on the other hand has been controlled by the anguished uncertainties of the narrator in the context of which Nanga is an unmitigated villain. Abruptly, we are freed from these uncertainties and confronted with Nanga's straightforward account: "He was once my pupil. I taught him ABC and I called him to my house to arrange for him to go to England. Yes, I take the blame." Unencumbered by ideals or principles, Nanga sees everything in terms of personal loyalty and mutual self-interest. We get a glimpse of the narrator's crises of inertia and ineptitude from his point of view, and we understand his contempt.

At the same time, of course, we witness the meeting from Odili's point of view. In the logic of his development this is the moment for the grand gesture which will at last point out to the people the corruption of their leaders. In place of the withdrawn and skeptical schoolmaster of the opening chapter we have the experienced participant who is no longer on the defensive either in his private or public life. In the perspective of his values the meeting looks quite different. When Nanga jeeringly offers him the microphone ("Come . . . and tell my people why you came"), Odili knows this is his opportunity:

"I come to tell your people that you are a liar and. . . ." He pulled the microphone away smartly, set it down, walked up to me and slapped my face. Immediately hands seized my arms, but I am happy that he got one fairly good kick from me. He slapped me again and again. . . . The roar of the crowd was now like a thick forest all around. By this time blows were falling as fast as rain on my head and body until something heavier than the rest seemed to split my skull. The last thing I remembered was seeing all the policemen turn round and walk quietly away. (xiii)

This is the climax of the novel, and we are encouraged to see it from the two extreme points of view represented there. For Nanga, immersed in the roughhouse of politics, Odili's act is both ludicrous and trivial and presumably confirms all his suspicions of the educated hybrids who ought to leave politics to the professionals. But from the more familiar point of view of the narrator this moment is the culmination of an ambition nurtured and matured throughout the novel. His idealism, now tempered by experience, has led him to perform this one selfless public act, unthinkable at the beginning of the novel.

While the narrator is in hospital, the novel ends in the confusion of political melodrama. Max is killed by an election jeep belonging to Chief Koko, one of Nanga's ministerial colleagues, who is in turn shot and killed by Eunice, Max's girl friend. Fighting then breaks out between the bodyguards. Nanga tries to disband his private army, which goes on the rampage. In this state of anarchy the prime minister cynically reappoints his old cabinet back to office. The thuggery becomes so extreme that the army stages a coup and locks up the Government.

Odili is at the same time recovering from a broken arm and a cracked skull. The anarchy into which society is declining corresponds to the crisis of his illness:

I remember the first time I woke up in the hospital and felt my head turbanned like an Alhaji. Everything seemed unreal and larger than life and I was sure I was dreaming. In the dream I saw Edna and my father and Mama standing around my bed. I also saw, through a gap in the screen, two policemen. But the only thing that was immediate and in focus was that pressure trapped inside the head pounding away in a panic effort to escape. (xiii)

The gesture of denunciation was the end as well as the culmination of Odili's attempt to enforce his ideals in society. He recovers

consciousness in a world beyond political redemption where the
only realities are those of personal affection. When the military
coup overthrows the Government he refuses the easy consolation
of ascribing it to the will of the people. The only ethic is that of
the national cake.

No, the people had nothing to do with the fall of our Government.
What happened was simply that unruly mobs and private armies having tasted blood and power during the election had got out of hand
and ruined their masters and employers. And they had no public reason
whatever for doing it. Let's make no mistake about that. (xiii)

In this political turmoil, in the midst of which Nanga is arrested
trying to escape disguised as a fisherman, Odili at last commits
himself fully to his personal relations. Edna's covert sympathy and
support turn out to be an index of her true feelings, so that when
he insists she succumbs and acknowledges she had never wished
to marry Nanga. Public events come to his assistance. After
Nanga's convenient arrest, the opposition to the marriage from
Edna's father crumbles. Finally, politics provides the means of
paying back all the money Nanga had spent on Edna's education:
"I had already decided privately to borrow the money from
C.P.C. funds still in my hands. They were not likely to be needed
soon, especially as the military regime had just abolished all political parties in the country . . ." (xiii). This is a new realism with
a vengeance. For the moment we wonder if a new Nanga is in the
making; the extent of the irony is difficult to assess. Perhaps it is
that amid the final welter of hypocrisy and selfishness Odili knows
that everything is subordinate to his love for Edna. There is hope
here as well as disillusionment, and this is reflected in Odili's final
mature diagnosis of the society in which he lives.

Despite the military coup Odili knows that everything has remained the same. The fickle public has deserted the deposed leaders—"Chief Koko in particular became a thief and murderer"—
and again switched its allegiance in the service of self-interest.
The murdered Max has become overnight a hero of the revolution. Now Odili understands the full, disturbing significance of the
story of Josiah the trader: in this political context the story is utterly irrelevant. No matter how many shining, monumental ges-

tures are made, the gap between the traditional social ethic and the national cake ethic will not be bridged.

When his father, musing piously on the reason for Koko's downfall, repeats once more the refrain of the novel—"Koko had taken enough for the owner to see"—Odili objects. He has just been to visit Eunice, Koko's murderer, in jail:

My father's words struck me because they were the very same words the villagers of Anata had spoken of Josiah, the abominated trader. The owner was the village, and the village had a mind; it could say no to sacrilege. But in the affairs of the nation there was no owner, the laws of the village became powerless. Max was avenged not by the people's collective will but by one solitary woman who loved him. Had his spirit waited for the people to demand redress it would have been waiting still, in the rain and out in the sun.

The politicians may take over tribal and village trappings to prove that their present roles are a continuation of traditional ones. But however much regalia is displayed, however many times the radio is called the National Crier, there is a disastrous fracture between the morality of the village and the political affairs of the nation. The narrator ends the novel by pointing to this, not as a sudden revelation, but as a truth which has now been experienced.

As the narrator seeks to diagnose the events in which he has been involved, the significance of Josiah's eventful career again becomes evident. Outlawed by the village, Josiah quickly became one of Nanga's most trusted henchmen in a regime which reversed village values, "a regime in which you saw a fellow cursed in the morning for stealing a blind man's stick and later in the evening saw him again mounting the altar of the new shrine in the presence of all the people to whisper into the ear of the chief celebrant." The "altar of the new shrine" is, of course, the election platform, and Josiah is informing the "chief celebrant" Nanga that a heretic, Odili, is present.

With this new religion in power and the laws of the village powerless, justice has to be left to individuals acting alone. Max was avenged in the only way possible, by someone who loved him. Private loyalties become the ultimate values in the absence of public moral sanctions. This is how the narrator's disillusioned political idealism and his private alienation have realigned

themselves by the end of the novel. In his final sentences he draws
the extreme contrast between public and private values. Against
the background of self-interest created by political anarchy, any
gesture of love or loyalty is of inestimable value. This is why the
dead Max is "lucky":

And I don't mean it to shock or to sound clever. For I do honestly believe that in the fat-dripping, gummy, eat-and-let-eat regime just ended
—a regime which inspired the common saying that a man could only
be sure of what he had put away safely in his gut, or in language ever
more suited to the times: "you chop, me self I chop, palaver finish";
. . . in such a regime, I say, you died a good death if your life had
inspired someone to come forward and shoot your murderer in the
chest—without asking to be paid. (xiii)

Here at the end, the author clearly endorses the depressing final
analysis of his mature narrator.

 Achebe began with the premise that the politician's role is inevitably divided. He must serve both the constituency which has
elected him and the Government of the country as a whole. This is
a difficult task at any time, but in the novel's anonymous African
state which is a conglomeration of local loyalties it is virtually
impossible. These loyalties are too strong ever to be transcended
by the needs of the country as a whole. This fracture between
local and national interests is dramatized very effectively in the
opening hostilities between the two main characters: the alienated young graduate who, having jettisoned his "primitive loyalties," despairingly compares the politics of his own with those of
other countries, and the successful, middle-aged politician who,
having abandoned his youthful ideals in the pursuit of power, can
with great facility translate the affairs of state into the immediate
interests of himself and his constituents.
 In the working out of this relationship Achebe's bitterness is
turned against the minister who masquerades as a man of the
people. His charade is the final betrayal of the communal ethic
which has been subjected to a variety of pressures in the previous
three novels. Other characters like Okonkwo and Ezeulu were
baffled by conflicting loyalties within the clan: Nanga is the first
to play his two loyalties off against each other with charming,
coldblooded calculation so as to exploit both and fulfil neither.

Parading the trappings of tribalism in the villages, Nanga can pretend to represent his constituency, but the people no longer have control over their leaders. When he leaves the village he is free to follow his own interests in the anarchy of national politics. If he is attacked in the constituency he can always provide another slice of the national cake; if he is accused of political immorality by the intellectuals he can label them European stooges and demand more and quicker Africanization. By the end of the novel, Nanga's very success in the constituency, his bonhomie, his rapport, have come to be an index not of his humanity but of his hypocrisy.

In the final analysis, the story of Josiah the trader must be seen as a parable which anticipates the final destruction of a way of life which has been celebrated with pride, affection, and concern throughout the novels. Josiah steals the blind man's only support, his stick, to concoct a *juju* medicine which will turn his already exploited customers into "blind buyers of his wares." He is stopped and punished by the villagers in the one effective social gesture in the novel. But his national counterpart, Nanga, is rewarded for *his* crime. He has stolen from the constituency its traditional ethic, its only guide in the complexity of the modern state. He has turned this against the people by cynically corrupting it into the ethic of the national cake. Now they are completely dependent upon him, their representative, for their welfare and survival. What was once their strength has become their weakness, for this man operates in the sphere of national politics where they can neither understand nor control him. "In the affairs of the nation there was no owner, the laws of the village became powerless." The traditional reciprocal relationship between leader and people has become a parody of itself and no longer is it true to say that "no man ever won judgement against his clan." The only language the villagers now understand is that of self-interest, and they assess their representative in his own terms, by the amount of loot he brings back to the constituency. In their apathy and cynicism the people have become the blind buyers of the politicians' wares.

CHAPTER 6

Conclusion

THE pattern of *Things Fall Apart* to which Achebe returns in *Arrow of God* is tragic and ironic. In each case, the complex web of relationships by which the clan lives, balancing its obligations and adapting to changing circumstances, is disrupted by the ambition of a strongminded individual. Both Okonkwo and Ezeulu chafe under the checks and balances of traditional Ibo life and by simplifying the tribal ethic seek to give freer rein to their ambitions. All they succeed in doing is to crystallize certain endemic weaknesses which undermine the clan from within just as an alternative religion is offered from outside. In each case it is a clash between a flexible, tolerant society which believes in balance and compromise and a single-minded, authoritarian character who, unable to live the fluctuating dialectic of the Ibo, demands consistent principles of action. The tragedy is that the impressive qualities of Okonkwo and Ezeulu seek this particular form of expression at the moment of the clan's greatest danger. The irony is that the protagonists by destroying the resilience of their societies to absorb the new challenge have frustrated their own ambitions within these societies.

The results can be seen in the two novels with contemporary settings. Here the values and customs of Europe and Africa have become inextricably tangled without forming any kind of stable synthesis. Achebe presents two extreme reactions to this dilemma. Obi in *No Longer at Ease* tries desperately to create a consistent life out of his double heritage and is quickly destroyed by its contradictions. Nanga, on the other hand, moves nimbly and unscrupulously between his two roles of tribal chief and cabinet minister and, until he overreaches himself, enjoys considerable success amid the general confusion and cynicism. All that we are left with at the end of *A Man of the People* is the narrator's credo of personal loyalty. We began with the gentle rhythms of the communal life of Umuofia; we end with the individual's desperate search for values in a disintegrating society.

This is the direction of Achebe's exploration of his major themes. What makes this exploration memorable is not, of course, any general statement we might extract from the novels but the accumulated impact of particular scenes and situations. These in turn are dependent upon Achebe's deployment of the resources of English to embody African experience. There is an inevitability about the language of the novels which should not blind us to Achebe's originality. The wise ancestral narrative voice of *Things Fall Apart* gradually loses its calm confidence in the face of the advancing strangers and finally capitulates to the acts of sacrilege it is incapable of describing. This is a triumph of style in the same way as the contrast between the panache of Nanga's pidgin and the narrator's Received Standard English takes us effortlessly to the heart of *A Man of the People*. Then there are the other varieties of English in the novels which are used by the author to cover the whole kaleidoscope of African and European attitudes—the polysyllabic jargon of the politicians, the stiff-upper-lip rhetoric of the colonial administrators, the extempore prayers of the converts with their admixture of African proverb and Christian doctrine, the demotic English of the servant and the court messenger.

But above all else it is Achebe's representation of the speech, the idioms, the proverbs of the Ibo still secure in their traditional way of life which stays in the memory. With complete conviction he persuades us that this is how his people spoke, thought, and viewed their world. To do this he has had to create a form of English with an African coloration. He has done this so successfully that, by a strange reversal, his Ibo characters establish their speech as the norm against which the language of the colonialists, the white men, seems bizarre and unnatural. The spare, supple English which represents Igbo has a metaphoric immediacy, but it is clear that the idioms and images are not those of colloquial English. Achebe hints in a variety of ways at the presence of another, African language behind the English modifying and at the same time enriching it in accordance with the needs of his characters. Yet it does not sound like a translation from Igbo. The English has taken on African contours without losing its flexibility; it ranges freely from the oracular utterances of the *egwugwu* to the irreverent asides of the villagers. And this form of language establishes itself as firmly as the traditional way of life it expresses; any departure from either is viewed with misgiving. Here, on the elusive level of language, Africa and Europe meet once more, and the novelist's divided heritage, which he has celebrated with pathos, amusement, and anguish, finally becomes his greatest strength.

Notes and References

Preface

1. "The Novelist as Teacher," *Commonwealth Literature,* John Press, ed. (London, 1965), pp. 204–5.

Chapter One

1. Joseph Conrad, *Heart of Darkness,* ch. ii.
2. *Ibid.,* ch. ii.
3. Leo Africanus, *The History and Description of Africa,* trans., John Pory, ed. Dr. Robert Brown (London, 1896), Vol. I, p. 187.
4. Useful discussions of these ideas are to be found in: Paul Bohannen, *Africa and Africans* (New York, 1964); Michael Crowder, *The Story of Nigeria* (London, 1966); Philip D. Curtin, *The Image of Africa; British Ideas and Action, 1780–1850* (Madison, 1964); M. Mahood, *Joyce Cary's Africa* (London, 1964); Paul Fordham, *The Geography of African Affairs* (Harmondsworth, 1965); James S. Coleman, *Nigeria: Background to Nationalism* (London, 1958).
5. O. Mannoni, *Prospero and Caliban; the Psychology of Colonization,* trans. Pamela Powesland (New York, 1964).
6. Chinua Achebe, *Arrow of God,* ch. xi.
7. I am indebted to the following works: Daryll Forde and G. I. Jones, *The Ibo and Ibibio-speaking Peoples of South-eastern Nigeria* (London, 1950); Margaret M. Green, *Ibo Village Affairs* (London, 1947); S. Leith-Ross, *African Women: A Study of the Ibo of Nigeria* (London, 1939); Margery Perham, *Native Administration in Nigeria* (London, 1937); Victor C. Uchendu, *The Igbo of Southeast Nigeria* (New York, 1965).
8. Jean-Paul Sartre, "Orphée noir," in *Anthologie de la nouvelle poésie nègre et malagache* (Paris, 1948), p. xx. Quoted in Waulthier, pp. 38–39.
9. "English and the African Writer," *Transition,* IV, 18 (1965), 29.
10. "Chinua Achebe on Biafra," *Transition,* VII, 36 (1968), 31–37.

Chapter Two

1. Throughout, numbers in parenthesis refer to the chapters of the following editions of Achebe's novels: *Things Fall Apart* (London, 1958), *No Longer at Ease* (London, 1960), *Arrow of God* (London, 1964), *A Man of the People* (London, 1966).

Selected Bibliography

Not a great deal has been written about Achebe. He is invariably included in generalizations about the West African novel, but apart from book reviews, there has been little detailed criticism of his novels. The following brief list contains most of what has been written. In addition, there are three useful bibliographies covering the general area of African literature: Janheinz Jahn, *A Bibliography of Neo-African Literature from Africa, America, and the Caribbean*, New York: Praeger, 1965; John A. Ramsaran, *New Approaches to African Literature*, Ibadan: Ibadan University Press, 1965; and Barbara Abrash, *Black African Literature in English Since 1952*, New York: Johnson Reprint Corporation, 1967.

PRIMARY SOURCES

ACHEBE, CHINUA. *Arrow of God*. London: Heinemann, 1964.
———. *Chike and the River* (juvenilia). London: Cambridge University Press, 1966.
———. *A Man of the People*. London: Heinemann, 1966; New York: John Day, 1966.
———. *No Longer at Ease*. London: Heinemann, 1960; New York; McDowell, Obolensky, 1960.
———. *The Sacrificial Egg and Other Short Stories*. Onitsha: Etudo Ltd., 1962.
———. *Things Fall Apart*. London: Heinemann, 1958; New York: McDowell, Obolensky, 1959.

———. "Chike's School Days" (story), *Rotarian* (April, 1960), 19–20.
———. "Uncle Ben's Choice" (story), *Black Orpheus*, 19 (1966), 45–47.
———. "The Voter" (story), *Black Orpheus*, 17 (1965), 4–7.

———. "English and the African Writer," *Transition*, IV, 18 (1965), 27–30.
———. "The Novelist as Teacher," *Commonwealth Literature*, John Press, ed. (London: Heinemann, 1965), pp. 201–5.

————. "Where Angels Fear to Tread," *Nigeria Magazine*, 75 (1962), 61–62.

SECONDARY SOURCES

BANHAM, MARTIN. "The Beginnings of a Nigerian Literature in English," *Review of English Literature*, III, 2 (April, 1962), 88–99.

BEIER, ULLI, ed. *Introduction to African Literature*. Evanston: Northwestern University Press, 1967; London: Longmans, 1967. A collection of critical essays, including Irele's essay on Achebe (below) and some general discussion of fiction.

EDWARDS, PAUL, AND DAVID R. CARROLL. "Approach to the Novel in West Africa," *Phylon*, XXIII, 4 (Winter, 1962), 319–31.

GLEASON, JUDITH ILLSLEY. *This Africa: Novels by West Africans in English and French*. Evanston: Northwestern University Press, 1965. An intelligent, wide-ranging critical discussion of the West African novel.

————. "Out of the Irony of Words," *Transition*, IV, 18 (1965), 34–38. Includes a brief discussion of *Arrow of God*.

IRELE, ABIOLA. "The Tragic Conflict in Achebe's Novels," *Black Orpheus*, 17 (1965), 24–32.

JONES, ELDRED. *Review of English Literature*, V, 4 (October, 1964), 39–43. Review of *Things Fall Apart*.

————. *Journal of Commonwealth Literature*, I (September, 1965), 176–78. Review of *Arrow of God*.

LAURENCE, MARGARET. *Long Drums and Cannons: Nigerian Dramatists and Novelists 1952–1966*. London: Macmillan, 1968. Includes a balanced, enthusiastic estimate of Achebe.

LINDFORS, BERNTH. "The Palm Oil with which Achebe's Words are Eaten," *African Literature Today*, No. I (1968), pp. 3–18. A thorough survey of Achebe's use of proverbs.

MOORE, GERALD. *Seven African Writers*. London: Oxford University Press (Three Crowns Book), 1962. Good introduction to Senghor, David Diop, Camara Laye, Amos Tutuola, Mongi Beti, Ezekiel Mphahlele, and Achebe.

————. *Transition*, IV, 14 (1964), 52. Review of *Arrow of God*.

MPHAHLELE, EZEKIEL. *The African Image*. London: Faber, 1962; New York: Praeger, 1962. An ambitious attempt to examine the cultural implications of literature in Africa.

NWOGA, DONATUS. "The *chi* Offended," *Transition*, IV, 15 (1964), 5. An objection to Shelton's article below.

OBUMSELU, BEN. "The Background of Modern African Literature," *Ibadan*, 22 (June, 1966), 46–59.

POVEY, JOHN. "Contemporary West African Writing in English," *Books Abroad*, XL, 3 (Summer, 1966), 253–60.

REED, JOHN. "Between Two Worlds: some notes on the presentation by African novelists of the individual in modern African society," *Makerere Journal,* 7 (1963), 1–14. Shrewd and suggestive speculation on recurrent themes.

SENANU, K. E. "The Literature of West Africa," *The Commonwealth Pen.* A. L. McLeod, ed. Ithaca: Cornell University Press, 1961, pp. 167–84. Brief comment on *Things Fall Apart.*

SHELTON, AUSTIN. "The offended *chi* in Achebe's Novels," *Transition,* III, 13 (1964), 36–37.

TIBBLE, ANNE. *African/English Literature; A Survey and Anthology.* London: Peter Owen, 1965; New York: October House, 1965.

TUCKER, MARTIN. *Africa in Modern Literature. A Survey of Contemporary Writing in English.* New York: Ungar, 1967. Includes a brief survey (pp. 83–93) of Achebe's four novels and a useful bibliography.

WALI, OBIAJUNWA. "The Individual and the Novel in Africa," *Transition,* IV, 18 (1965), 31–33.

WAULTHIER, CLAUDE. *The Literature and Thought of Modern Africa.* Trans. Shirley Kay. New York: Praeger, 1967; London: Pall Mall, 1966. The best background study.

Selected Bibliography

[illegible reversed/offset text]

Index

155